Hidden Victims

Hidden Victims

The Sexual Abuse of Children

Robert L. Geiser

Beacon Press   Boston

Grateful acknowledgment is made to the American Journal of Nursing Company for permission to use the material in chapters 16 and 17 which is based on an article, "Sexual Disturbance in Young Children," by Robert L. Geiser and Sister M. Norberta, which originally appeared in *MCN, The American Journal of Maternal Child Nursing,* May/June 1976, Vol. 1, No. 3.

Beacon Press books are published under the auspices of the Unitarian Universalist Association.

Published simultaneously in Canada by Fitzhenry & Whiteside Limited, Toronto

(hardcover) 9 8 7 6 5 4 3 2
(paperback) 9 8 7 6 5 4 3 2 1
Library of Congress Cataloging in Publication Data

Geiser, Robert L.
    Hidden Victims.

    Bibliography: p.
    Includes index.
    SUMMARY: Discusses the possible causes and aftermath of the sexual misuse of children resulting from incidents involving incest, rape, prostitution, and other activities.
    1. Child molesting—United States. 2. Child abuse—United States. 3. Incest. [1. Child molesting. 2. Child abuse. 3. Incest] I. Title.
HQ72.U53G43   364.1'53   78-73853
ISBN 0-8070-2954-3
ISBN 0-8070-2955-6

This book is for an eleven-year-old foster child who died in September 1978 of a subdural hematoma, the result of child abuse. Besides being brutally abused physically, she may have been sexually molested as well. Perhaps this book will contribute to the day when other children will not share her fate.

Robert L. Geiser
Wellesley, Massachusetts
October 1978

"Since this is a phenomenon that thrives and proliferates in darkness, we need to open windows and doors and promote open public discussion of the topic. Increased public awareness is best stimulated by people who care enough to snatch every opportunity to arouse society's consciousness of the child victim of sexual abuse. Only then will the public sanction, so vital to identifying and assisting these children, be forthcoming."

Suzanne M. Sgroi
"Sexual Molestation of Children," in *Children Today*

Acknowledgments

I would like to thank my friend and colleague Harold M. Wolman, M.D., for his critical reading of the manuscript and his many helpful comments and observations.

My thanks also to Nick Groth for his willingness to share so generously with me his considerable experience in the field of child sexual abuse, especially his work with sex offenders, and for inviting me to present some of my material with him and his colleagues at a professional symposium on the sexual abuse of children.

Lastly, my thanks to the unsung heroes behind most writers, the librarians, in particular, the helpful staff of the main branch of the Wellesley Free Library for obtaining resource material for this and my other books. My thanks also to the Wellesley College Library, the library at the University of Massachusetts, Boston, and to a number of other area libraries for allowing me to use their facilities.

Contents

Introduction
The Last Frontier

Social problems have an uncanny ability to survive most attempts to remedy them. Their first line of defense is to hide from public awareness and then later to spring onto the scene as full-blown crises. As a result, everyone wonders why a problem wasn't recognized until it reached crisis proportions.

Actually, looking back, one can usually find that there were voices warning the public about particular social problems in their early stages. Look, for example, at pollution, the decimation of our natural resources, racial unrest, energy shortages, and the declining quality of education. But people pay little attention to warnings precisely because the situation is not yet a crisis or does not personally affect them. The public labels as an alarmist anyone who cries "Wolf" before the wolf actually puts in an appearance.

Social problems remain hidden from public scrutiny through a variety of techniques. One is the ability to camouflage themselves, to appear to be something other than what they are. For example, poverty is often attributed to laziness. It becomes, then, the natural result of an unwillingness to work. To attack the social problem of poverty, ways are devised to force lazy people to work. Hence, most remedies for poverty are ineffective because the problem has more to do with economics and emotions than laziness. While the war is waged against the wrong enemy, poverty thrives.

Progress cannot be made in solving disguised social problems until they are labeled by their right names. In order for that to happen, someone has to be able to overcome a mind set and dare to think the unthinkable—or the obvious.

Child Abuse

Like most social problems, child abuse is not new but has been around for a long time. It had, however, gone underground before the early 1960s and was not in most people's consciousness. In fact, the biggest single obstacle to its detection was the unwillingness of physicians to entertain child abuse as a possible diagnosis in cases of children treated for broken bones, bruises, internal injuries, burns, skull fractures, and so forth.

These injuries to young children were serious, sometimes life-threatening. If the children did not die, they often survived with brain damage, retardation, or severe crippling. The parents or other adult caretakers who brought the children for medical care were often reluctant to explain the injuries and attributed them to accidents. True, some of the injuries could have been the result of accidents—which is the largest single cause of death for children in the United States. But some physicians found it difficult to reconcile the nature and extent of the injuries with the parents' accounts of the accidents. How does a two-year-old "accidentally" receive numerous cigarette burns on his genitals, or an infant the criss-cross welts on his back, buttocks, and legs that look as if they were inflicted by a belt or chain?

The alternative to accepting these injuries as accidental was to think the unthinkable—that the children were being abused by their caretakers. Most professionals involved could not do that. Even if they thought it, the possibility of being sued for saying it stilled their tongues. The injuries, maimings, and deaths went on.

Then, in 1962, in an article in the *Journal of the American Medical Association,* C. Henry Kempe and his associates put the unthinkable into words.[1] Some of the physical injuries of children were not caused by accidents at all, they asserted, but were in fact the result of physical assaults by adults on children. The "Battered-Child Syndrome" came into being.

Once Kempe and others made the shift from accepting the injuries as accidental to seeing them as the result of abuse, the problem was forced out into the open. Things began to change.

In the next decade, other professionals published articles and books confirming Kempe's work. Hospitals created a new diagnostic category, Trauma X, to label suspected child abuse cases. The connection between subdural hematomas and fractures of the long bones of the arms and legs was recognized as a typical injury in child abuse cases. Pediatric X-ray techniques were perfected to detect previous healed or healing fractures of the bones, a finding that suggested chronic abuse. Federal money became available, and researchers turned their attention to child abuse. Studies on incidence, epidemiology, social class, characteristics of abusing families, and other variables appeared in the literature. The popular press and magazines featured articles on child abuse.

The initial reaction of the public to this information was what one would expect. There was, once again, a marked resistance to accept the unthinkable. It was inconceivable to many people that adults could batter or severely neglect children. Perhaps it could happen in isolated cases, but certainly only rarely. Besides, the adults involved in such behavior were probably crazy. No sane adult could ever do such a thing. Ordinary people, like you and I, would never physically harm a child. Through an array of defense mechanisms, people warded off a confrontation with their own deeply buried and unacceptable impulses.

Slowly the evidence in support of the unthinkable piled up and shattered most of the mistaken notions. Child abuse was found to be not a rare occurrence at all. It occurred in all social classes and the abusers were not just the poor and the mentally ill.

By 1967, the public finally had its consciousness raised to a point where efforts were made to stem the tide of child abuse. That year, all fifty states, plus the Virgin Islands and the District of Columbia, had child abuse reporting laws. Puerto Rico joined the others shortly thereafter. Although the laws varied in different jurisdictions, generally they made the reporting of suspected child abuse mandatory for certain professionals, such as physicians, teachers, social workers, psychologists, police, and nurses. The laws granted these professionals immunity from being sued should their reports turn out to be unfounded. Some laws were not restricted to professionals but required any citizen to report suspected cases of abuse. In some instances, the laws provided stiff criminal penalties for failure to report. All over the country, hot lines sprang up to facilitate anonymous reporting of child abuse.

Public and private welfare agencies developed child abuse treatment teams to offer counseling and help for abusive parents. Health organizations held workshops and seminars on the topic of child abuse. Self-help groups of former abusive parents, such as Parents Anonymous, were founded. New York's Odyssey Institute established a residential facility where abusive parents could learn how to parent adequately. In 1974, a National Center on Child Abuse and Neglect was created in Washington, D.C., by the Child Abuse Prevention and Treatment Act of 1974 (PL93–247). Congress appropriated $85 million for the treatment of abused children and their parents. In 1976, the first National Conference on Child Abuse and Neglect was held in Atlanta, Georgia.

Although great strides have been made in dealing with the problem of child abuse, it is still pandemic. It is painfully clear that the problem is more widespread than has been previously thought. The number of cases of child abuse reported under the new laws has soared, increasing 10 to 15 percent per year. In the United States as a whole, in 1967, there were only 7000 cases of child abuse reported. In 1976, the number was over the half-million mark. Estimates by HEW's National Center on Child Abuse and Neglect place the true occurrence at over the one million mark, at least double the half-million cases reported in 1976.[2] One researcher studying violence estimated from his studies that at least one child in thirty-three runs the risk of abuse or neglect.[3]

A conservative estimate of the number of deaths from child abuse each year places the number at over 2000. One national expert, Douglas Besharov, director of the National Center on Child Abuse and Neglect, recently said, "If you had a communicable disease that struck as great a number of children, you'd say you had an epidemic on your hands."[4] More children die each year from abuse than from any *single* infectious disease. Child abuse is the number five killer of children, exceeded only by accidents, cancer, congenital abnormalities, and pneumonia. The United States may well lose the war on child abuse, just as it lost the War on Poverty some years ago.

Child Abuse as a Symptom   One of the reasons we fail to wipe out child abuse is that we deal with symptoms and rarely attack the root causes embedded in our society. We deal with child abuse after it happens, but do little preventive work. For example, many of the danger signs that should alert us to potential child abuse are known: marital strain, poverty, parental immaturity, parents who were themselves abused as children, social isolation, overwhelmed mothers, and the interaction between social class and social stresses. But there has been little or no increase in programs to deal with these factors. There is a great need for expanded counseling services for marriages in trouble, financial help for the poor, day-care centers for working mothers, homemaker services for overwhelmed families, support services for families in trouble, extended family networks, parenting education courses, and scores of other services. Until these programs are a reality, child abuse will not be controlled.

Most telling of all, there is no indication that we are willing to abandon the philosophy of violence that pervades our society. One example: a large majority of American parents and elementary school teachers still strongly favor corporal punishment in the schools. In 1977, the Supreme Court heard arguments on the first corporal punishment case involving spanking in the schools. *(Ingraham* v. *Wright).* The Court did not take this opportunity to put an end to institutionalized violence against children. Instead, the high court denied students constitutional protection against physical force and any constitutional right of due process to determine whether the punishment was justified or not. The April 1977 decision came in a close five to four vote of the Court and was a major defeat for the Children's Rights movement. The only recourse students now have in the case of severe or arbitrary punishment is to sue for damages at the state or local level. That, however, is not going to end beatings.

Violence against children breeds violence. Sirhan Sirhan, James Earl Ray, Lee Harvey Oswald, and John Wilkes Booth all had histories of abuse and neglect in childhood.[5] Clinical experience shows many abusive parents were themselves battered as children. Violence remains an accepted part of the child-rearing philosophy in America, and there is currently an upsurge of the "get tough with kids" philosophy. Coercion and cruelty have never made for good parenting, good teaching, good child care, or for that matter, good children. As long as society condones the use of force by parents and institutions, there will continue to be a child abuse epidemic.

Types of Child Abuse As we come to know more about child abuse and neglect, we realize that the battered child is the last stage in what is actually a spectrum of maltreatment of children. Vincent Fontana has formulated the "Maltreatment Syndrome" in his book *The Maltreated Child.*

At the opposite end of the spectrum from the estimated 200,000 cases of severe physical abuse lies the broad area of child neglect. This includes the failure-to-thrive baby and those children deprived of normal maternal care through neglect. The neglect may be physical—

inadequate food, shelter, and clothing—or may be specific—not receiving medical treatment or preventive care. Severe neglect is capable of producing retardation in children: infants who do not receive adequate physical stimulation, food, or care can and do develop severe retardation, which is largely irreversible. Estimates as to the size of this group place the number of neglected children in America at around 700,000.

A third point on the spectrum is psychological and/or verbal abuse. The child who is continually abused verbally—called names and insulted or rejected by an adult—is also a maltreated child, not physically battered perhaps, but battered in spirit and in self-esteem. There are no accurate figures on the size of this group.

Another point on the maltreatment of children spectrum is sexual abuse. This has been called the last frontier of child abuse, and for good reason. We are presently at about the same point historically with regard to sexual abuse of children that we were in the early 1960s vis-à-vis physical abuse. Professionals are only now daring to say the unthinkable, and the public is just beginning to hear what the professionals are saying. The increased openness of society to discuss sexual matters has helped create a more favorable climate in which to explore this topic.

The public reaction to the issue of sexual abuse is a repeat of their earlier attitudes about the battered child. They find it difficult to believe adults could sexually abuse a child. Certainly it must be a rare phenomenon, occurring only in poor families, and perpetrated by monsters or mentally ill adults. The reaction I received from people who asked me what book I was currently working on was either a shudder or an exclamation of disgust or both. This was followed by the question, "But is that really so much of a problem?"

The answer to the question is, "Yes. It is a major social problem." Sexual abuse of children is not rare. The National Center on Child Abuse and Neglect estimates that 200,000 children a year are sexually molested. Some experts estimate that the number of sexually abused children may equal or exceed the number who are physically battered. Like physical battering, sexual abuse is not confined to the poor, nor are any but a handful of offenders psychotic.

It is the purpose of this book to bring together what is currently known about the sexual abuse of children, to try to understand why it happens, and to explore what can be done about it. Granted the topic is not a pleasant one. This book is written not to entertain but to inform. Only by daring to verbalize the unthinkable can we ever hope to deal effectively with a social problem that presents a serious physical and mental health threat to a segment of America's children.

Defining Sexual Abuse

David Walters, in his book *Physical and Sexual Abuse of Children,* defines sexual abuse of a child as "the utilization of the child for sexual gratification or an adult's permitting another person to so use the child."[6]

The definition is nonspecific and probably circular. Sexual gratification is something usually inferred and almost impossible to prove. It is assumed that sexual behavior gratifies sexual needs. There is much to suggest, as we shall see, that sexual gratification is *not* the dominant motivation in many so-called sex crimes, and also may not be the major motivation for either offenders or victims in cases of sexual abuse of children.

Other writers have preferred to talk about the sexual *misuse* of children, rather than *abuse.* They consider the term *misuse* more accurate and desirable for a number of reasons:

Sexual abuse is construed as a legal term, while misuse expresses a mental health viewpoint. The issue for the mental health of children is not the things done to them which are legal crimes, but rather any inappropriate and premature sexual stimulation, criminal or not.

Sexual abuse forces us to think in dichotomies—adult abusers versus child victims. In truth, both parties, and usually other family members as well, are victims. The child is not always the victim, but may be a willing participant, often to satisfy nonsexual needs of his or her own.

Some children who have been involved in sex with adults do not feel as though they have been abused. Sexual abuse is a pejorative term, an adult's value judgment of the situation, and leads to thinking in terms of punishment of the offender. Misuse suggests a normal process gone astray and leads more naturally to treatment rather than punishment.

Abuse implies an exclusive relationship between abuser and victim, which is often not the full picture. Sexual abuse of a child is often a symptom of family dysfunction. The term misuse is a reminder of the need to study the entire system of human interrelationships. The consequences of sexual misuse will show up somewhere in this system—as physical and/or behavioral symptoms in the child or as psychic distress in other family members.

The term abuse constricts thinking about solutions. Since it leads to the dyad of abuser/victim, it suggests a solution of separating the child from the abuser. As we are coming to realize, however, the separation of a child from his or her family is an extremely stressful action. In most cases it causes more harm than good. It breaks up families rather than supporting and strengthening them. While it may seem that separating a child from the family is in the child's best interests, it is necessary to take a long, hard look at the old warning—first, do no harm.

Brandt and Tisza propose this definition of sexual misuse: "Sexual misuse of a child is the exposure of a child to sexual stimulation inappropriate for a child's age, level of psychosexual development, and role in the family."[7] It is important to realize that "inappropriate" varies with families, ethnic groups, and sociocultural context.

The above definition of misuse is the one I prefer to use in this book. I shall use the terms abuse and misuse interchangeably, but the reader should remember that the definition referred to is the broader one of misuse which, like the concept of physical maltreatment, refers to a spectrum of behavior. Misuse ranges all the way from adult exhibitionism at one end, through fondling, genital contact, sodomy, penetration of any orifice of the child, intercourse, and finally, to the most extreme violation, rape.

There is little argument that sexual penetration, intercourse, and rape are clearly abusive of children. However, there is not such universal agreement about where misuse may shade into variations of normal behavior. How, for example, does one distinguish parental displays of affection from excessive fondling? Some families are much more physically demonstrative than others. Parental nudity around the house might be sexually stimulating to some children at certain ages in some families. In other families, the nude display of the body might not be overstimulating. This underlines the need to evaluate the child's total environment in order to understand the meaning of the sexual behavior involved.

Incidence of Sexual Abuse

The true incidence of both child abuse and sexual misuse of children is largely unknown. All experts in the field agree that sexual

misuse is grossly underreported. In the case of sexual misuse, conservative estimates are that there are at least two or three unreported
cases for every one that is reported.

Compared to other classes of crimes, sex crimes of all types are
generally underreported. It is not difficult to understand why this
should be so. In our culture, sex is still a sensitive subject. People do
not talk easily about sexual behavior, especially when it involves
children. There is still a strong public attitude of disapproval toward
the victim of a sex crime, as if such a thing doesn't happen to decent
people. In adult rape cases, for example, the victim is often badly
treated by the police, courts, and lawyers.

Sexual misuse of children often involves other family members,
as in the case of incest. Sometimes preference is given to the protection of the family as a unit rather than to the individual child. A
mother may fail to report the sexual misuse of her daughter for fear
that her husband will be taken away from her. Other cases are not
reported because the child or adult does not know to whom to turn
for help.

Solid statistics on sexual abuse come from *reported* cases. Beyond
that, one can only guess at how many unreported cases there are. The
major sources of reported cases are police and court records, hospitals,
mental health clinics, and child abuse hot lines. Some of these sources
deal largely with criminal acts and do not cover misuse that may not
be criminal in nature. There is further bias in the fact that the legal
system and the public health network are more likely to deal with poor
people than the middle- and upper-class offender.

In spite of the limitations on such data, it is informative to look
at some representative figures:

In a recent article on sexual abuse of children, *Ms.* magazine
stated, "One girl in every four in the United States will be sexually
abused in some way before she reaches the age of 18."[8] Unfortunately
Ms. did not give a reference for this figure. It may well have come from
Kinsey's book, *Sexual Behavior in the Human Female,* in which he
reported that one in four of the white, middle-class females he interviewed revealed an unwanted preadolescent sex experience of some
sort with an adult male.[9]

Another estimate is that 150 of every 100,000 children under the
age of sixteen are victims of a sexual abuse that is reported to the
police. If that rate is translated into specific terms, it would mean an
expectation of 3000 cases yearly in New York City and about half
that number in the metropolitan Washington, D.C., area.[10]

An interesting 1956 study of 1800 college students in New England showed one-third had been sexually abused as children.[11] These were mostly middle- and upper-class children. Further, the percentages were almost equal for both male and female students. The last is of interest in view of the fact that statistics on victims of reported sexual abuse show only 5 to 10 percent of all child victims as male. Sexual abuse of male children is probably grossly underreported.

A national study of child neglect and abuse reporting for 1975, based on at least twenty-nine states, showed sexual abuse accounted for 10.6 percent of all validated cases of child abuse and neglect.[12]

In Connecticut, in 1973 and 1974, sexual abuse comprised 9 to 11 percent of all reported cases of child abuse. In 1973, Connecticut passed a child abuse reporting law with a stiff fine for mandatory reporters who failed to report cases known to them. The next year, reported child abuse cases nearly tripled, while sex abuse cases more than doubled.[13]

In California, in 1968, sex abuse cases comprised 14 percent of all child abuse cases reported. That figure was probably lower than it should be since cases of both physical and sexual abuse were tabulated under physical abuse alone.[14]

During a six-year period ending December 1973, 189 cases of physical abuse were seen at the University of Texas Medical Branch Hospitals. Of these, 12 percent (twenty-two cases) were of sexual abuse.[15]

Based on these figures, a reasonable estimate of sex abuse cases would place them at 10 to 20 percent of all reported cases of child abuse. However, experts such as Vincent DeFrancis of the American Humane Association in Denver, Colorado, say that the incidence of sexual abuse is equal to or many times greater than that of physical abuse. Time, increased public awareness of the problem, and better reporting procedures may someday tell us if he was right.

PART I
Sexual Misuse of Female Children

Chapter I
What Is Rape?

WARNING!

If you are contemplating rape (and the majority of rapes are planned), be sure to check the statutory penalties for this crime in your state. Usually the most severe penalties are reserved for raping your neighbor's *wife* (20 years to life). The punishment is less severe (up to 10 years) for raping your neighbor's *child*. The penalty is even less (up to five years) for raping your *own* child. If this offends you, try raping your wife. In most states, this is not considered a criminal offense at all!

Legally, rape is sexual intercourse with a female without her consent, by force or threats of force. (Until recently the law never considered the possibility that anyone other than a female could be raped.) Usually only penetration is necessary to commit rape; ejaculation does not have to occur. Statutory rape is sexual intercourse with a female under the age of consent, often fourteen years of age, but this may vary in different states.

Molestation consists of various forms of sexual contact between an adult and a child short of actual intercourse. It may be fondling and caressing of the body or genitals, digital penetration of the vagina or anus, genital contact without penetration, or masturbation.

Depending upon various state laws, anal and oral sex may be considered rape, child molestation, or sodomy. The last term is ambiguous. Sodomy may include oral and/or anal sex. It may cover intercourse with animals, although bestiality is also used to refer to this practice. Sodomy sometimes refers only to sexual behavior between members of the same sex, but in some jurisdictions it includes "unnatural sexual relations" between members of the opposite sex. In many states, oral and anal sex between a man and a woman, whether married or not, is a criminal act. If these laws were enforced, a considerable portion of the American population would be sexual criminals.

Rape, in the legal sense of sexual intercourse, certainly occurs with female children to a degree greater than most people would imagine. Of about equal frequency, however, are molestations of female children which stop short of penetration and intercourse. Some mental health professionals consider these contacts to be rape also. To the less legal mind, rape has a broader definition than sexual intercourse. To health professionals, rape is any nonconsenting sexual contact.

It is not always clear, in reading mental health literature on child rape, exactly what behavior is involved. One can be more confident reading legal literature on rape that actual or attempted sexual intercourse was involved. The reader should keep this semantic problem in mind. I have tried to use rape to refer to actual intercourse and molestation to refer to other types of sexual contacts, but it has not always been possible to be consistent in this usage. Some authors have added further confusion to the problem by referring to oral or anal rape.

One tends to assume in rapes involving adults that the object was forced sexual intercourse. It is not always clear with children that this was so. In considering sexual contacts with children one needs to think in terms of a wider variety of sexual activities than is usually the case in sexual behavior between adults.

Some writers in the area of child sexual abuse include incest as a form of rape, which it certainly can be. In this book, however, incest is considered separately in Part II because the family pathology involved warrants closer scrutiny. Sexual offenses against male children, also a form of rape, are covered separately in Part III because they raise some very different issues.

What Rape Is Not—the Mythology of Rape

It matters not whether the victim is an adult or a child, the vast majority of rape offenders are males. It is also other males who write the rape laws, investigate and prosecute the crimes, judge the guilt, and administer the punishment. In our male-dominated society, there are some very mistaken notions as to what rape is. People generally see rape as a sex crime. After all, goes the reasoning, an act involving the sex organs must be sexually motivated. Most rape experts agree, however, that rape is not a sexual crime. It is a crime of violence, an assault upon the integrity of another person using sex as a weapon.

In his work with sex offenders, Groth distinguished two categories of adult rapes based on whether the major underlying motivation for the attack was anger or power.[1] The anger rape, which comprised about 35 percent of his 133 adult rape offenders, was characterized by violent physical assault on the victim. The purpose of the assault was to humiliate, abuse, and degrade the victim. Anger, hatred, and contempt were the primary emotions expressed. Far more force than was necessary was used in the assault, and the offender expressed revenge and retaliation against the victim for what he felt were the rejections and hurts inflicted on him by women in his past.

The balance of the rapes (65 percent) were power rapes. These were premeditated and planned assaults. Threats were used against the victim more often than a weapon or physical brutality. The object was to overpower the victim and to put her in a helpless position where she could not refuse his sexual advances. Erotic arousal stemmed from these feelings of strength and power over the helpless victim.

Groth concluded that rape was a sexual *deviation,* that is, sexual behavior in the service of nonsexual needs. Because of the threat to the physical or psychological safety of another, such behavior is deviant. None of Groth's 133 offenders had to rape for the purpose of sexual satisfaction. There was no effort on the part of the offenders to negotiate a consenting sexual relationship with their victims. Prison did little to help these men since over half (63 percent) of the recidivists in his sample showed an increase in force and aggression in their assaults over time. None showed a decrease.

Groth felt that rape served the same function as a symptom, i.e., it expressed a conflict in the offender, helped defend against anxiety, and partially gratified or discharged an impulse. The act of rape was a symptom of a developmental defect in the offenders. Rapists had failed to achieve an adequate sense of self-identity and self-worth. They had been frustrated in their efforts to achieve a masculine image. Under conflicts and pressures in the rapist's later life, especially in sexual relationships where he may have felt especially victimized and inadequate, he resorted to active and assertive actions to attempt to regain a sense of mastery over his life.

Rapists, according to the male fantasy, are supersexed individuals. Groth found, however, that in at least a third of his offenders, the men experienced some type of sexual dysfunction during the sexual assault.[2] Most frequent were impotence and inability to ejaculate. Only a quarter of his sample showed no clear evidence of any sexual dysfunction during the rape. (One implication of this is that the absence of sperm does not mean that a woman wasn't raped. In almost half of a sample of ninety-two rape victims, sperm tests were negative. Groth suggests this may have been due to a sexual dysfunction on the part of the offender.)

The rapist seeks power and dominance over women, and the feelings he expresses are hostile, often violent, destructive urges toward women. One has only to read accounts of rapes, such as those in *Rape! Victims of Crisis* by A. W. Burgess and L. L. Holmstrom to appreciate the hostility in both the rapist's actions (forcing the victim into degrading acts) and his verbalizations (insults and swearing).

Rape is also assumed to be brought about by sexual deprivation. According to this view, rapists are sexually frustrated individuals. Yet studies show that two thirds of rapists are married and have sexual relations regularly.[3] Rapists are rarely overwhelmed by sexual impulses. If anything, they may have a less than average interest in sex.

The problem for the rapist is not so much the control of his sexual impulses as it is the control over his hostility and aggression. Rapists are called sexually dangerous persons, but it is not the sex that is dangerous, it is the violence. It is not sexual intercourse that harms the victim, but the violence with which it is done.

Rape is further misunderstood as being an impulsive crime. The truth of the matter is that rape is rarely an impulsive crime but is premeditated in most cases. One study shows that 71 percent of all rapes are planned in advance. This is even more true of gang rapes, which are 90 percent preplanned.[4]

A number of consequences result when rape is seen as a sexual crime rather than as an aggressive one. Note the following:

1. *One looks at the victim to see if she enticed the rapist.* Perhaps she was seductive, flirtatious, or wore provocative clothing. In a study of 100 adult rape cases in Dade County, Florida, spanning a twenty-two-month period in 1970–1971, the county medical examiner separated out twenty-one cases in which he thought the rape could be traced to a place where the initial mechanism, leading up to the rape, was set in motion. He says, "What dalliance, what flirtation, what social foreplay went on at the dance or the bar to whet the male's appetite is anyone's guess, but the thought occurs, had the woman not been at any of those places, a sexual attack would not have followed. One can almost use the legal phrase 'contributory negligence.' " (The same logic applied to bank robberies would hold that it is the bank's

fault for being robbed because it insists on keeping money there.) At another point, the same author says, "Three victims were wearing hot-pants suits. Today, many righteous citizens are commenting, 'No wonder they're being raped; look how they're going around.' " The author adds, however, that "Dress in these particular cases, appeared to have been immaterial," but leaves open the possibility that in other cases dress may be relevant in provoking attack.[5]

2. *The past sexual history of the victim becomes relevant in court.* If you can show the woman was promiscuous or a prostitute or not a virgin, you strengthen the case for the defense. The prevailing male attitude seems to be that only virgins get raped because they don't know any better. A woman with sexual experience must know what it is all about, so she can't be innocent of the man's intentions. Some women's groups against rape are pushing for state and federal legisla-tion which would make a woman's past sexual history inadmissable in court in rape cases.

now happening

In August 1978, the Connecticut Supreme Court, acting on an appeal of a 1974 rape conviction, ruled that a rape victim cannot be forced to testify about her sexual history because it is irrelevant to a defendant's guilt or innocence. The convicted rapist's attorney held that the victim's sexual history was relevant in proving whether the woman had consented to have sexual relations with his client. The court disagreed and upheld the conviction.[6] The decision was a step in re-specting the privacy of rape victims.

3. *The victim's past psychiatric history becomes relevant for the defense.* After all, what would you expect from an emotionally un-stable victim but to consent to sex and then turn around and cry "rape"? If the victim is a child/teen ager, the defense will try to show a history of behavior problems or antisocial behavior. "She's nothing but a runaway," sneered one policeman about a teen ager who had been raped. The unstated assumption is that runaways are bad kids and probably have loose morals.

4. *The issue of consent becomes important.* If the woman gave consent and then changed her mind, who can blame the male if he raped her? After all, it is dangerous to sexually arouse a man and then refuse to have sex. If the emphasis is on rape as an aggressive crime, then consent is irrelevant. No one has a right to attack another person physically. No one asked if the woman consented to violence. (Is the male assumption that sex is always a violent or aggressive act?) With children, the fact that force rarely has to be used often leads to the erroneous impression that the child consented. This obscures that fact that a child cannot legally consent to sexual acts.

5. *People are prevented from seeing that rape victims can be other than females.* "You mean men and boys get raped, too?" one startled

individual asked. "Is that possible?" A sixteen-year-old boy was picked up hitchhiking by two women. They held a knife on him and forced him to have oral sex and intercourse with them. After taking his wallet, they let him out alongside the road. The boy reported the attack to the police. He was met with disbelief. ("What the hell are you complaining about? You're lucky to get it.") The police reluctantly acted, however, and caught the two women. The prosecuting attorney refused to take the case to court for fear of being ridiculed. Ordinarily, one doesn't associate children with sex, so it is difficult to believe that child rape exists as well.

6. *It becomes difficult to accept the fact that a woman can commit rape.* After all, women are not supposed to be aggressive about sexual matters. Under the laws of most states, only men commit rape. For example, in many states it is statutory rape if a *man* engages in sexual relations with a woman, not his wife, who is less than fifteen years old.

In April 1977, the U.S. District Court in New Hampshire declared that state's law unconstitutional because it applied only to men. In October of the same year, the Court of Appeals agreed. The case went to the U.S. Supreme Court, which declined to review it, raising doubt over the constitutionality of statutory rape laws in other states because they do not apply equally to men and women.[7] New Hampshire repealed its law and replaced it with a neutral law. The new law held that a man *or* a woman could be prosecuted for engaging in sexual relations with persons less than fifteen years of age of either sex. In 1974, Massachusetts made the same change in its law, but set the age at sixteen.

A recent newspaper article reports the case of an offender, a twenty-two-year-old Massachusetts woman, who is charged with raping a boy under sixteen on three separate occasions. The woman is the mother of a twenty-two-month-old son and a seven-month-old girl. She is already serving a nine- to twenty-year term in prison. She and her twenty-three-year-old husband were convicted of forcibly raping a fifteen-year-old girl. The woman also has two other charges pending against her—one involving the alleged rape of a fifteen-year-old boy, and the other allegedly committing an unnatural act on a fourteen-year-old boy.[8]

7. *Male and female offenders are treated differently.* A male who has sex with a female child is a rapist or child molester. A woman who has sex with a male child will probably be viewed much more tolerantly. It is likely to be called sex education, and if she is charged, it will be a lesser offense, such as contributing to the delinquency of a minor.

A recent example in New Mexico involved a twenty-three-year-old housewife and a fifteen-year-old consenting boy. The woman was charged with contributing to the delinquency of a minor, but the state appeals court dismissed the charge. One judge said that "intercourse with a young boy is nothing more than sex education essential and necessary in his growth toward maturity and subsequent domestic family life."[9]

The other judge reasoned that New Mexico defines delinquency as an act that would be criminal in an adult. Since New Mexico had repealed penalties for consenting sex between adults, the act was not delinquent. The state supreme court, however, on its own motion, reversed the appeals court and reinstated the indictment.

Seeing rape as a sexual crime leads to being sidetracked with issues of consent, sexuality, promiscuity, and immoral behavior. Tremendous strides might be made in treating rapists if the focus was on their deviant angry behavior rather than on their sexual behavior. All other issues fade when one sees rape for what it is, a crime of violence, using sex as a weapon, that can be committed by males as well as females against adults or children of either sex.

Chapter II
Child Rape—Realities and Myths

The incidence of child rape is staggering:

Nationwide, one out of every five rape victims is under twelve years of age.[1]

Of 2190 women and child victims of sex attacks in Washington, D.C., between 1965 and 1969, 13 percent were under nine years of age; 23 percent were between ten and fourteen; 22 percent were between fifteen and nineteen. The age range of victims was six months to ninety-one years.[2]

Of seventy-one rape cases in Hartford, Connecticut, in 1976, more than a third were under sixteen years of age.[3]

Fifty out of every 100 rapes reported in Philadelphia, Pennsylvania, happen to people under sixteen years of age, and twenty-four of those to children under thirteen years of age.[4]

In November 1973, a rape prevention research project in Denver, Colorado, reported that 24.5 percent of all sexual assaults by adults were committed on children.[5]

The first year of a rape treatment project at Boston City Hospital in Massachusetts found thirty-seven of 146 victims (28 percent) to be children.[6]

The Rape Treatment Center at Jackson Memorial Hospital in Miami, Florida reported that 34 percent of its victims/patients of rape were fifteen years or younger. During 1975, a total of 768 victims were treated there.[7]

A rape occurs on the average of every nine minutes throughout the United States. A child rape occurs once every forty-five minutes.

There are some distinct differences between rapes involving children and those involving adult victims.

20

It is more likely that the offender is known to the child.

The majority of attacks on children take place indoors, 60 percent either in the victim's or the offender's house.[8]

Children, as compared with adult and adolescent victims, are least likely to be the object of physical violence. All forms of physical force are less common with children than with other age groups. According to one study, no physical force was used in 54 percent of the cases.[9]

Child assaults take less time than adult rapes. Sixty-nine percent took less than fifteen minutes versus only 18 percent with adolescent victims. Almost a third of adult rapes took over an hour.[10]

Most child assaults involve only one attacker (about 80 percent in one study).[11] Statistics for adult rapes show 73 percent with only one attacker.[12]

There is a wider range of sexual offenses involved in attacks on children. One study reported 30 percent fondling and caressing; 20 percent involving penile-vaginal contact with no penetration; 7 percent using oral sex; 12 percent involving rectal intercourse (vaginal intercourse was reported less frequently than this, but children may be confused about the differences in their bodies); and 20 percent using masturbation and vaginal penetration other than by the penis.[13] Another study of 175 child assaults found half involved only sex play, 38 percent involved penetration, and 13 percent involved both sex play and penetration.[14]

These stark realities may shock many people because they contradict widely held notions about child rape. These popular ideas are not based on fact, but are actually fantasies that exist precisely because people are unaware of the facts. In the usual educational model, ignorance is replaced by knowledge. But with emotionally loaded topics like the sexual misuse of children, it is not that simple. Before they can learn, adults must first be de-educated, that is, disabused of the fantasies they harbor concerning the problem.

Myths about Child Rape

There are many fantasies, or myths, about sexual abuse of children. Following are some of the most common:

1. *Children who are raped are primarily older, teen-aged children.* This is simply not true. Victims as young as two months have been raped. A seventeen-month-old child died of asphyxiation in her crib. An

autopsy revealed semen in her mouth and throat. A nineteen-year-old babysitter was responsible.[15]

The mean age of sexually abused children (not all of whom are rape victims) tends to be around eleven years. Children's Hospital National Medical Center in Washington, D.C. reports that approximately 10 percent are under five years of age; slightly more than a third are from six to ten years old; and about 55 percent fall into the eleven to fifteen year age range.

In a ten-year study of all child victims of sexual offences examined at the University Institute of Forensic Medicine in Copenhagen, Denmark, 13 percent were under five; 30 percent between five and nine; and 57 percent between ten and nineteen. Nearly a third of all these children were victims of rapes or attempted rapes.[16]

2. *Children who are raped are retardates.* It is true that retarded children (along with foster children) are a high-risk group for sexual abuse but the vast majority of child victims are not retarded. Any child can be a potential victim, given the right set of circumstances, regardless of the child's age, race, intelligence, social class, or neighborhood.

3. *The child victim comes mainly from the lower socioeconomic family.* Family income and social status are not related to sexual abuse. They are related, however, to an increased likelihood of the abuse being reported to a public agency rather than to a private practitioner.[17] A study in Denver found child rape and molestations were spread throughout the city and its suburbs and not confined to economically depressed areas of the city. This was not true for adult rapes, where six out of 125 census tracts in the downtown area accounted for one third of the rapes.[18]

4. *Rape victims, either adults or children, are the objects of racial attacks.* Of 1500 rape cases in Philadelphia, 90 percent took place between members of the same racial group.[19] The metro fact sheet from the Dade County, Florida, area shows 87 percent of the rape cases involved victims and offenders of the same race.

5. *Children are molested on playgrounds and other outdoor places.* In fact, the child is in more danger in her own home and in the homes of friends of the family. About three fourths of child rapes take place indoors and one third occur in the child's own home. Child offenses other than rapes, such as molestation and exhibitionism, occur in the warmer summer months when children do tend to be outdoors. When a child is raped outdoors, the offense still tends to occur fairly near either the victim's or the offender's house. Most of the child offenses occur during daylight hours, with the majority between noon and 8:00 P.M. and an additional one third from 8:00 P.M. to midnight.[20]

6. *The child is in greatest danger from a total stranger.* In fact, the

child is raped or molested more often by someone she knows. This is even more true for the younger child. The Children's Hospital National Medical Center states that the child knows the offender in 80 percent of the cases. With older children, this may be reduced to half. The difference probably reflects the older child's mobility, while the younger child spends more time at home and with people she knows.

The classic 1965 study by Vincent DeFrancis of 250 cases of child sexual abuse in Brooklyn-Bronx found the offender known to the child 75 percent of the time.[21] In a study of twenty-five court-referred child molesters, only six percent were total strangers to the child.[22] The Center for Rape Concern in Philadelphia reports that in 80 percent of their cases, the offender was someone known and trusted by the child: neighbor, mother's boyfriend, relative, teen-age baby sitter, or an acquaintance of the family.[23]

7. *Sexually abused children are fairly evenly divided between young girls attacked by men and young boys attacked by women.* In fact, the vast majority (over 95 percent) of sex offenses are committed by men, including attacks on young boys. *Reported* cases of women molesting boys are rare, and female homosexual involvement with children is virtually never reported.

Some experts in the area take exception with these general figures. Some believe that boys are molested to nearly the same degree as girls in spite of the fact that in most reported studies males comprise only 5 to 15 percent of the victims. Others believe that assaults on children by women are increasing. Data on both of these questions are very difficult to find, and the picture at this point is far from clear.

8. *The sexually abused child is usually physically damaged because of the use of force in the sexual assault.* The use of physical force in sexual contacts with children is rare. Less than 5 percent of the cases involve forced penetration with violent attack.[24] The child rapist/murderer is extremely rare. There are probably less than ten child sex murders a year in the United States.[25] They are a terrible tragedy when they do occur, but they do not represent a *major* threat to the well-being of children. Cases of extreme violence are likely to involve adults who are mentally defective, psychotic, or alcoholic. Groth found only eleven out of 137 sex offenders he studied to be of this sadistic/violent type.[26]

This does not mean that the child rapist does not use verbal threats, some physical force, or threats to kill the child if she tells anyone about the assault. In assaults on adult victims, force is used in at least three fourths of the cases and weapons in at least a third.[27] Weapons are rarely used with children. In a study of 175 males convicted of child sexual assaults, Groth found in half the cases that the predominant method of engaging the victim in the sex act was through intimidation or threat. This meant physically overpowering the child or threatening to harm her if the victim resisted. The next most frequent approach (30 percent of the cases) was through seduction/enticement where victims were bribed, tricked, or pressured into sex through rewards and/or reassurances that the behavior would not be harmful to the child. Only 20 percent of the cases involved a brutal attack on the victims with specific intent to hurt them.[28] Assaults on teen-agers are more like adult rape cases. Physical injury occurs about one fourth of the time, and weapons are used in one-half the cases. The rest of the assaults involve the use of fists, choking, and threats.[29]

Attempts at physical penetration of a child, either digitally or genitally, may be painful and may lead to injury. The Voigt study reports less than 1 percent of the victims under fifteen years of age had been *severely* injured. About a third of the children under nine years of age had genital injuries, but most of those were trivial.[30] There was a tendency for children to become more withdrawn after an assault.

In 1975, ten children who were victims of sex abuse, out of a total of 132 abuse cases, were treated at the St. Louis Children's Hospital. The oldest, thirteen years old, was pregnant; three girls aged eight, three, and three, had gonorrhea; four girls aged eleven, nine, four, and three had vaginal discharges; a five-year-old girl complained of painful urination; and a three-year-old boy had facial bruises and a tear in the anal region. Of some 2000 sex attack victims in Washington, D.C., twenty-four were admitted to a hospital for severe injuries, six of these were children. Eleven other children were sutured for lacerations in the emergency room. One four-year-old child had syphilis.[31] (The issue of mental damage from a sexual assault will be dealt with in the next chapter.)

9. *Sex abusers are rapidly prosecuted, convicted, and sentenced.* Only one rapist in twenty is ever arrested, one in thirty is prosecuted, and only one in sixty is ever convicted.[32] This is the lowest conviction rate for any violent crime. While these figures are for adult rapes, the situation is not much better for child rapes.

With children, prosecution is a lot more common if the abuser is a stranger (assuming he is caught in the first place). Since most abusers are not strangers, prosecution is, in fact, rare. Many cases are never reported to the police. For those that are, conviction is difficult because children make unreliable witnesses, and many parents refuse to put their children through the horror of a public trial.

10. *The offender suffers more from public exposure of sexual abuse than the child.* Contrary to popular belief, this is often not so. Hysterical parents may accuse the child of lying, of bringing on the abuse by her own actions, of trying to break up the family (when the abuser is a relative), or of disgracing the family (presumably by being a victim). In some cases, peers may stigmatize the child.

11. *The abuser is the stereotyped Dirty Old Man.* The proportion of child rapes committed by senile men is minuscule. In a number of studies on rapists and child molesters, the average age of the men is in the early thirties. In the Voigt study, nearly half the offenders were in the twenty-five to thirty-nine-year-old range, and only six were over forty years of age.[33] The mean age of 175 child sex offenders studied by Groth was thirty-one years.[34]

There has also been an increase lately in the number of rapes committed by young persons in their late teens and early twenties.[35] In about half the rapes of teen-age children, it is not uncommon to find the victim and offender within ten years of each other.

To many people the rape of a child is a terrible thing. But they feel if it doesn't physically harm the child, the child will get over it quickly with few lasting scars. The extent to which that is another myth is the subject of the next chapter.

Chapter III
Traumatic Effects of Rape

Rape is precipitated by an internal crisis in the psyche of the offender and results in an external crisis in the life of the victim. Burgess and Holmstrom have identified a cluster of symptoms typical of adult victims as they react to the external crisis of rape. This collection of symptoms is called the *rape trauma syndrome.*[1] Child victims of rape and molestation also show reactions typical of the rape trauma syndrome.

Burgess and Holmstrom divided the rape trauma syndrome into an acute phase, marked by acute disruption and disorganization in the victim's life-style, and a long-term phase, in which the victim tries to reorganize her life.

In adults and children, the acute phase may be either a controlled reaction, calm and composed but with subdued affect, or an expressed reaction, with a wide range of feelings of shock, disbelief, fear, anxiety, restlessness, anger, crying, and so forth. There are often disturbances in eating and sleeping patterns as well as bodily complaints of soreness, itching, bleeding, or discharge from a body orifice.

Burgess and Holmstrom report that the long-term process with adults and children often involves dreams and nightmares, sometimes of the victim committing an act of violence, such as murder; changes in life-style, such as not going out alone or turning to the family for support; and phobias, perhaps a fear of crowds or of being alone.

Peters reports his child victims showed fewer changes in behavior than his adolescents or adults.[2] Still, 20 percent of his victims ate less than usual and 31 percent reported difficulties in sleeping. Nightmares were common in 20 percent of the cases, with the child often crying out in her sleep.

Peters mentions that 11 percent of his child victims did not feel safe any longer where they lived; 32 percent showed more negative feelings for men they knew; and 34 percent were more negative toward strange men. Nearly half of his cases showed an increased fear of being out on the streets. Ten percent of the school-aged children stopped going to school after the incident, developing in effect a school-phobia (the fear and anxiety are displaced from the rape onto the school situation).

Burgess developed a separate category to describe some child rapes, which she called "accessory-to-sex."[3] This is, I believe, an unfortunate choice of words, but by it she means that the child was pressured into sex activity by an adult who stood over the child in a power position, and then further pressured the child into keeping the act secret. The victim experiences this added burden—of keeping the secret—as fear. Because they do not report the rape to anyone, many of these children live with fear and other psychological upset for long periods of time.

Burgess and Holmstrom reported that of their child victims, most reported mild or moderate to severe symptoms.[4] Very few children escaped with no symptoms.

Physical symptoms in children beyond the ones already mentioned include painful urination, enuresis, encopresis, and conversion symptoms, such as abdominal pain. There is always the possibility of venereal disease, vaginal/rectal infections, and, in older children, pregnancy.

Behavioral symptoms run the gamut from general irritability to learning and school behavior problems, acute withdrawal, depressive symptoms, delinquent acting-out, running away, and, in older children, prostitution. Behavior which is specific to the trauma sometimes occurs and may include excessive masturbation and other autoerotic behavior, excessive sexual curiosity and play, or overtly seductive behavior toward other children and adults.

The Time-Bomb Effect of Child Rape

Peters has called child rape a psychological time bomb.[5] In his practice, he saw a number of adult women whose sexual disorientation or psychosis was directly traceable to a childhood rape incident. A child who was apparently little affected at the time of the rape stores up psychological dynamite that may explode at some crucial point in her psychosexual development in later life. Among the crucial points where an explosion can take place are courtship, marriage, childbirth, and a rape or attempted rape in later life.

Peters related one case of a girl, raped forcibly by a male baby sitter when she was four years old. The baby sitter was the mother's lover. When the mother found out, she was more concerned about her own relationship with the boyfriend than with her daughter's welfare. She begged the girl to keep the rape a secret from her father because she said the father might kill the baby sitter.

The child misunderstood what mother told her and interpreted it to mean that she herself had done something bad. She grew closer to her father, who was a kind, intellectual, and safe person. Years later, as an adult, the woman was able to relate to men only on an intellectual, nonsexual level.

Another example of the time-bomb effect was the three-year-old girl who was assaulted by a male baby sitter. About three months after the incident, mother suddenly remembered and told her psychiatrist that at seven years of age, she, too, had been assaulted by a male baby sitter. The mother had exposed her child to the same trauma that she had experienced as a child.

Amy Katan, a psychoanalyst who has treated a number of women who were raped as children, said that some of her patients showed a dangerous tendency to repeat the traumatic incident in various ways throughout their lives—a phenomenon other analysts have noted with their patients. In particular, Katan's patients tended to expose their own children to the same experience they had endured by not protecting them properly.[6]

Most of Katan's patients had been attacked at an early age and were orally raped. Katan pointed out that a young child who is directly overstimulated sexually does not have discharge channels available. While the experience may at first have been pleasurable, it rapidly became painful due to the lack of discharge and this, in turn, stimulated aggression.

The most serious consequence of these early rapes, then, was not in the sexual sphere, but in a disturbance of the aggressive drive. Rape, since it closely combines aggressive and libidinal (loving) contacts, disrupted the normal fusion of the two drives. These women were fixated at the anal-sadistic stage, where destructive aggression never became tempered with warm, tender, and affectionate feelings.

All of these women had an extremely low self-esteem. They felt worthless, rarely achieved anything satisfying as adults, and couldn't succeed in life. The only way the women could escape these painful feelings was by identifying with men. They needed to see themselves as aggressive attackers, strong and powerful. If these fantasies of strength were disrupted, they were immediately plunged back into feeling like worthless victims. The women complained of never feeling that they were whole persons. They felt fragmented, caught in an eternal swing of ambivalent feelings, seeing themselves alternately as worthless and aggressive attackers. They also turned tremendous aggression against themselves.

With these early rapes, apparently it is not the premature sexual stimulation of the child that is so damaging, but the aggressive aspects of the attack. Virtually all children see and feel sexual behavior as basically aggressive. The mixture of pleasure and pain in the sexual attack, and the tremendous confusion it raises about people close to them who both love and hurt them disrupts children's ability to temper their normal aggression and sadism with loving and affectionate feelings. A child's destructiveness is not tamed but set free from this encounter, turning against animate or inanimate objects, or against the self. The developing ego is blown apart, unable to integrate, to make wholes out of the pieces. This is felt psychologically as not being a complete person. It translates into an inability to get along with other people or to become close to them because aggressiveness keeps getting in the way.

Aggression turned against the self may be acted out in being the chronic victim, in continually failing, in exhibiting delinquent/criminal behavior, in engaging in promiscuous sexuality, or in other types of self-defeating behavior. Directed against others, it may result in an inability to get close to men because of suspiciousness and anger; frigidity; sexual unresponsiveness; or an intense competitiveness and need to be in control. It may also be directed against one's own children in the aggression implicit in failing to protect them.

Critical Issues Raised by Rape

Rape raises certain critical issues for the victim and, especially when the victim is a child, for her family as well. The lives of the victim and the victim's family are disrupted by these issues.

One of the first issues is that of sexuality. Parents have to come to terms with the fact that their child is no longer sexually "innocent." The more the parents think their children are asexual creatures, the more traumatic will be the shattering of their supposed innocence. Most parents are initially worried about physical injury to the child. Once they have been reassured that no serious physical harm has come to the child, they then worry about emotional scarring. Prominent concerns are that the female child will avoid men or be turned off to sex as an adult. Parents need to know what happens to child victims of sex attacks in this respect. They also need to understand the importance of allowing the child to talk to a professional, and to them, about what happened. The worst thing the parents can do, besides being hysterical, is to urge the child to forget the experience and refuse to talk about it with her. This silence convinces most children that they have done something terribly bad, which has hurt and disappointed their parents.

As for traumatic effects on a child, the less frightening the incident, the less likely that there will be serious aftereffects. There is less trauma:

If it is a single attack rather than repeated assaults on a child.

If the attacker is a stranger, rather than a family member, friend, or neighbor—someone the child knows and trusts.

If the incident did not involve force or injury.

If actual penetration and intercourse did not take place.

If the child does not have to go through prolonged police questioning, legal proceedings, and courtroom appearances.

If the adults around the child react calmly to the incident and are supportive.

If the assault is reported to an adult rather than if the child tells no one, especially if the silence goes on for years.

If the child receives victim counseling and psychiatric help, rather than no emotional support in trying to understand the assault. Older children may have specific concerns about sex and may need help in distinguishing sexual assault from the loving, caring expression of sexuality in adult life.

A second issue raised for the child and family is dealing with the feelings of fear, outrage, anger, and guilt that affect both victim and family. Any traumatic event can shake a person's psychological sense of well-being. Victims of all types of crimes and accidents wonder why the event happened to them—if they were to blame, and how they could have prevented the incident. The feelings of vulnerability to harm raised in both victim and family can be overwhelming. Parents may feel guilty that they failed to protect their child, that they are bad parents, regardless of whether or not they realistically or reasonably could have prevented the attack. Some people even lose confidence in their ability to deal with future life crises.

A third and closely related issue is the feeling of powerlessness engendered by the rape. The child has been overpowered and has had her physical integrity violated by an adult. She may doubt her ability to defend herself in the future, or the ability of adults to protect her. Parents may feel that they and their children are completely at the mercy of outside forces, helpless to protect themselves.

Another issue for both victim and parents is embarrassment. Parents may not want neighbors, friends, or other family members to know what happened to their child. The child herself may be embarrassed that peers will find out what happened to her. This last fear may be related to the school-phobia that sometimes develops in school-aged children who have been sexually assaulted.

Many other reactions to a child rape are possible, depending upon the circumstances, the psychic structure of victim and parents, and their vulnerability to stress. The important point is that rape precipitates an emotional crisis in victim and family. The reactions to this stress can impair the mental health and functioning of both victim and family. Timely crisis intervention can help to prevent future emotional distress.

Chapter IV
Offenders and Treatment

According to the Center for Rape Concern in Philadelphia, in half of their cases of child molestation, the offenders had themselves been sexually abused as children.[1] The offenders were generally men with poor impulse control, and in half of the CRC cases, this was also compounded by an alcohol problem.

Men who molest children are described as not only inept in their sexual lives, but generally manage everything in life poorly. Men who turn to children as sexual objects can be classed in two types.

One is the fixated offender, whose psychosexual development appears to have been arrested in childhood, and who has been mainly interested in children as sex objects ever since adolescence. This group makes up what are commonly called pedophiles—lovers of children.

The second group is the regressed offenders, men who turn to children for sex when their adult relationships become complicated, unsatisfying, stressful, or anxiety laden. For example, a man who has never before molested children may do so when his wife is pregnant. Emotionally shut off from his wife, who is preoccupied with the changes going on inside of her body, he looks to children for love and affection. This type of man is usually a passive and emotionally dependent husband. At some point in their married life, his wife, because of some increased psychological or physical pressure on her, turns to him for emotional support. Overwhelmed by her needs and deprived of a wife who can meet his needs, he regresses.

Groth studied 175 males convicted of sexual offenses against children and found they divided almost evenly between fixated (eighty-three) and regressed (ninety-two) offenders.[2] He also found some interesting differences between the two groups:

32

The fixated offenders were younger (mean age, twenty-eight years) on the average than the regressed offenders (thirty-three years). In part, this is implied by the terms, since the regressed offender has to first establish an adult sexual orientation and then retreat from it while the fixated offender never does advance beyond a certain point in his psychosexual identification.

Only 12 percent of the fixated offenders had ever been married, while 75 percent of the regressed offenders were married.

The fixated offenders showed a preference for male victims (42 percent) over female (34 percent) or both sexes (24 percent), while the regressed offenders overwhelmingly chose female victims (71 percent) over male (16 percent) or both sexes (13 percent). This suggests that nearly half of the fixated offenders had an exclusive preference for boys.

In 83 percent of the cases, the fixated offenders were either complete strangers or else casually acquainted with their victims, while the regressed offenders were acquainted in less than half of the cases (47 percent). In the total sample, one third of the offenders were *complete* strangers to their victims.

It is rare to find child rapists who are mentally ill. The percentage of psychotic offenders is generally reported to be between 5 and 10 percent. That is not to say that offenders against children do not have emotional problems. They do, but not to the extent that it impairs their judgment and reality testing.

In one study which contrasted adult rapists with child molesters, the incidence of psychosis among pedophiles was very low, and that among rapists was even lower than in the general population. The study concluded that psychosis was not associated with either of these sexual offenses.[3]

The profile of child molesters suggests no particular psychiatric diagnosis for the group other than sexual deviation. Molesters are unlikely to have shown other criminal behavior in their past, and violence is not a feature of their activities. In a sample of 111 child molesters who had been referred for psychiatric evaluation by the courts, 9 percent were diagnosed as schizophrenic, 13 percent as mentally retarded, and 14 percent as manifesting organic brain syndromes. The most common secondary diagnosis for both the rapists and child molesters was alcohol or drug abuse.

Rapists are distinguished by being younger, on the average, than child molesters, and more likely to have had one or more prior incidents of violence in their histories. The psychotic rapist-killer, a favorite character in films and books, is fortunately rare in real life, but the violent history of the rapist is fact.

Joseph Peters, of the Center for Rape Concern (formerly the Sex Offender and Rape Victim Center) in Philadelphia, studied 224 probationed male adult sex offenders by means of an extensive battery of psychological tests.[4] Peters does not make clear how many offenders fell into each of the four groups—rapists, pedophiles, exhibitionists, and homosexuals—nor does he distinguish between rapists who chose adult victims and those who chose child victims. Still, some of his findings contrasting rapists with child molesters are interesting:

The mean IQ for pedophiles (94.5) was the lowest of the four groups, whose mean IQ was 97. One third of the pedophiles had IQs below 85.

All groups of sex offenders reported more symptoms of illness on a medical index than comparable groups of normals. The pedophiles scored highest on a somatic scale, indicating a large number of physical symptoms. This is related to a tendency to view themselves as inferior. Unable to attract adult women because of this felt inferiority, they turned to little girls for affection and sexual gratification.

The pedophiles showed considerable immaturity, strong dependency needs, much overall regression, and a feeling of phallic inadequacy. They were better able to restrain their impulsiveness than rapists.

Pedophiles showed less tendency to harbor latent homosexual impulses than the rapists. This may suggest that rapists are driven to sex assault by any situation that makes them feel feminine, weak, helpless, not in control, and so forth. By contrast, pedophiles under stress tended to become withdrawn and isolated. Pedophiles were also considerably more passive than rapists.

These findings underline the child molester's need to exercise authority and avoid rejection, making children appealing victims. Peters also notes that the aggressive component, so obvious in adult rapes, is not so clearly evident in child rapes. This does not mean it isn't there, but only that the child rape victim is less likely to experience the rape as a violent physical assault.

The child's vulnerability and helplessness make her or him easier to overpower and dominate by bribes, threats, intimidation, or mild force. It is usually not necessary to use extreme force, as often happens with adult and adolescent rapes. Sexual assaults against children in which violence is used are probably anger rapes, aimed at revenging some traumatic event that happened to the rapist as a child. Extreme violence with children is the mark of the sadistic offender who intends to harm the child.

The rapist is not interested in negotiating a consenting relationship with his victim. Where the adult rapist uses sheer force, the child rapist adds bribes and threats to his approach to the victim. By contrast, the child molester generally avoids violence and, if rebuffed by a child, may often turn to another child. He is interested in a consenting relationship with the child and often will select a victim he knows, if only slightly. He tends to identify with the child, whom he sees as loving, open, warm, and innocent. If a molester does harm a child, it is usually inadvertently or because he panics.

A Look at Treatment

The picture was dramatic. The man was lashed to an upright wooden stand, face downward. His back was covered with a sheet, with extra thick padding across his kidneys to protect them. He was wearing baggy pants. More than 100,000 people made up the noisy, screaming crowd that had come to the race course to watch the man be beaten with a wooden cane. The jail guard backed up and then ran and struck the man across the back. He did this fifteen times, with a cane soaked in mustard oil to increase the pain as the liquid seeped into the wounds. The crowd was not happy with the fifteen lashes. They wanted to see the man beaten to death.

That scene took place in Pakistan. The prisoner was a twenty-seven-year-old mill worker convicted of raping a seven-year-old girl. The man had lured the neighbor girl into his home with a promise of sweets. She required weeks of treatment in a hospital after the attack.

When the beating was over, the prisoner was carried on a stretcher to a truck that took him to the prison hospital, where he began his ten years in prison.[5]

A violent society is not interested in psychiatric treatment of offenders—it wants only punishment. In the United States, until the moratorium on capital punishment, rape was a capital offense in many states. At an earlier time, castration was the punishment for sex offenders. There are still those who call for this solution to the problem of sex offenses. A court in the United States recently offered a prisoner a choice between a lengthy prison sentence and castration for his sex crime. How castration cures violence is difficult to see. It is not even clear that it ends sexual impulsiveness.

Prison terms for rapists and child molesters do nothing to solve the problem either—prison only makes it temporarily impossible to commit a crime. Some rapists come out of prison more violent than when they went in. They certainly aren't cured. Brain surgery and drugs that render one impotent have also been tried as "treatments." They are themselves a violent response to violence.

A Novel Treatment for Rapists   "Stilling the Rage that Drives Men to Rape," read the newspaper headline.[6] The article recounted a unique treatment program at New Jersey's Adult Diagnostic and Treatment Center for sex offenders. The prisoners at the $7.2 million center which opened in 1976 are sent there for indeterminate sentences. They are not released until the staff and a private citizens' review board decide that they are well enough.

The program attempts to zero in on the urges that impel men to commit rape, sodomy, incest, and child molestation. A variety of programs are available, from videotaped group therapy sessions to individual therapy, patient-directed group therapy, and sex education courses.

The Center has 191 inmates, of which 70 percent are white. They are, as a group, greatly different from the usual prison population. Most of the men have worked steadily and are "family men" whose wives see them as good providers, good husbands, and good sex partners. They are sensitive, guilty men, troubled by a deep sense of inadequacy. Many had disruptive and abusive childhoods.

According to the Center staff, many of the men were sexually abused as children—most often between the ages of five and seven. This traumatic event has often been repressed, and the men have no conscious memory of it until therapy stirs things up, and the prisoners will suddenly remember an incident from childhood. For one, it was being fellated by his mother; for another, a long-term incestuous relationship with his sister. With memories come rage, anger, guilt, and pain. Often the anger is directed at their mothers, whom the men feel never gave them the care, nurturing, and concern they needed, but abused them instead. It is here one sees so clearly the connection between the violence done to them as children, and the violence they did to others as adults.

One rapist beat up on a dummy, calling it "bitch." At one point his hand flashed to his hip-pocket, pulling out an imaginary switchblade. He raised it high and just before plunging it into the dummy with killing force, he pushed the dummy away. The dummy was a stand-in for his mother. Instead of killing her in real life, he turned his great rage against mother-substitutes, his rape victims.

A middle-aged businessman who molested his twelve-year-old stepdaughter discovered his motivation: "I was dominated by my wife sexually and every other way. I wanted to dominate someone else."

There is evidence that the unorthodox treatment program works. The national recidivism rate for *all* prisoners is 70 percent. For sex offenders, it is about 60 percent. For the Center's paroled inmates, it is only 12 percent.

Shock Cure for Child Molesters In 1974, the maximum-security prison at Somers, Connecticut, was the scene of a controversial treatment program for child molesters. The program used electric shock and the principles of behavior modification.[7] The twelve-week therapy course involved fifteen repeated pedophiliac offenders. The convicted child molesters watched as pictures of naked children, taken from pornographic magazines, were flashed onto a screen. Each time a picture of a naked child appeared, the offender received a shock on his inner thigh. When the pictures were alternated with those of a naked adult woman, the prisoner received no shock.

The shock, produced by batteries, was of very low intensity—one-half a milliampere at 100 volts. It produced no pain, but rather a tingling, unpleasant sensation and the immediate desire to withdraw from it.

The procedure was aversive counterconditioning—an attempt to condition a negative (aversive) response to a stimulus that, because of prior conditioning, previously elicited a positive or approach response. At the same time, an attempt was made to condition a pleasurable response (no shock) to a stimulus (naked adult woman) that had previously elicited an avoidance response. In plain language, it was hoped that the prisoner would stop molesting children and turn to women for his sexual outlet.

In another aspect of the program, inmates were hypnotized and, in conjunction with the shock treatments, were taught to associate unpleasant or fearful thoughts or objects with pictures and thoughts of children. They were also taught to associate pleasurable thoughts with pictures and thoughts of adults. This procedure was covert sensitization—by associating repulsive imagery with children, it was hoped that the prisoner would no longer obtain pleasure in thinking of children.

The program was based on a punishment model in learning theory. It was quick, inexpensive, and apparently worked. Nine of the fifteen offenders in the program were paroled. Psychological tests for pedophilia and sexual deviation indicated significant changes in the inmates' personalities. At the time that the program was reported in the newspapers, none of the nine had been re-arrested for any crime. However, the longest any of the program participants had been out of prison was only eleven months.

"Children are not sexual objects to me anymore," one child molester said after his treatment. He claimed not to have dreams and nightmares about children any longer. "I couldn't have them if I tried," he claimed. "I want to lead a normal life and go back to my wife and son. I'm tired of jail." The man had served a total of sixteen years in prison in the last twenty-two years.

The Somers program came under heavy attack from the Connecticut chapter of the American Civil Liberties Union. They saw the program as a form of government thought-control. It was questionable that the program could be truly voluntary since the inherently coercive atmosphere of prison makes informed consent impossible. In addition, since participation in the program was linked with increased chances of parole, a subtle form of coercion was present.

The ACLU brought suit against the Connecticut Correctional Institute at Somers with the aid of three inmates who alleged that prisoners were denied parole unless they took part in the behavior mod program. The ACLU prevailed, and the Somers program ended.

With the Somers controversy, society found itself in the middle of a conflict over rights. How much coercion could be brought to bear on a prisoner to take a treatment that would "cure" him? Could one ever give voluntary consent in a coercive environment? What about the rights of children not to be molested by an offender? What about a person's right to treatment and release from confinement if a potential cure is available?

These are difficult questions. They weren't necessarily answered in the Somers case, but the courts will inevitably have to grapple with them in future cases.

PART II
Incest—Our Special Secret

Chapter V
The Nature of the Problem

Incest is an ugly word. Most people would prefer not to think about its meaning. Every state makes incest illegal, with penalties ranging from a fine and a year in prison to up to fifty years in prison. The public usually reacts with horror and disgust to accounts of incest. Yet, in spite of a strong taboo and legal sanctions against it, incest occurs every day to a greater degree than most people would imagine.

Incest is legally defined as sexual intercourse between persons so closely related that marriage is prohibited by law. The majority of cases involve parents who have sex with their children (mostly father-daughter) and incest between siblings (brother-sister). Mother-son incest is rare—there are very few reports in the literature—but it probably occurs with a greater frequency than realized. A study in West Germany reported only 4 percent of all incest cases involved mothers and sons. Another study of 200 court cases in Chicago found 164 cases of father-daughter incest, but only two cases of mother-son incest.[1]

Beyond the legal definition of incest there are three other types of sexual misuse of children, which, while they may not be legally defined as incest, are closely related to it and do share some common features.

The first type of relationship is becoming more common in America. Perhaps it could be called "psychological incest." It involves a violation not of a biological barrier, but of a psychological or emotional bond that exists between people who call themselves a family.

In recent years the divorce rate in America has risen sharply. There has also been a substantial increase in the rate of remarriage, with divorced individuals establishing second families. This new family may contain children who are neither blood relatives to each other nor blood relatives to *one* parent. Thus, a father may have sexual relations with his stepdaughter, which may or may not be legal incest, but which is psychological incest—the abuse by an adult of a parenting role. Any adult who fills the social role of parent and who has sex with a child in his "family" commits psychological incest. The most frequent occurrence outside of a marriage relationship is by the boyfriend of a divorced mother. Another example is the foster father/foster daughter sexual contact. The law might consider this child molestation or rape, but for our purposes it will be considered incest.

While the legal definition of incest involves sexual intercourse, it is important to realize that many sexual contacts between adults and children may not involve sexual intercourse. The second type of sexual misuse of children, which is incestuous because it occurs between family members, includes oral, anal and interfemoral contacts, mutual masturbation, digital insertion, petting, and touching of sexual organs.

Even in cases of incest as legally defined, it is most unusual for the sexual behavior to immediately begin with intercourse. There is usually a progression of sexual contact over a considerable period of time. Most commonly it begins with exhibitionism. This leads eventually to masturbation, mutual masturbation, and other fondling. If and when penetration does occur, the first attempt is usually oral. This is not so strange when one stops to consider the difference in size between adults' and children's genitals. The mouth is simply the largest orifice in a child.

The next step in the progression is likely to be digital penetration of the vagina or rectum, which may or may not be painful to the child. The final point of the progression is vaginal or anal intercourse. With female victims, the sex play may go on for years, and intercourse may not be actually attempted until around puberty. This is the usual pattern, but that does not mean that intercourse isn't attempted in younger children. There are cases on record of children under a year, some of only a few months, who have been victims. Needless to say, with a child this young, the result is often physically harmful, possibly fatal.

The third type of incestual relationship to be included here are those sexual contacts that technically (legally) don't involve intercourse since that term usually refers to sexual behavior between opposite sexes. Specifically, this third category consists of same sex contacts—between father-son, mother-daughter, or like sex siblings.

Father-son contacts are the more common of this type of parental abuse. One example: A four-year-old boy died from rectal intercourse, the victim of a male baby sitter and his own father.[2] A study in West Germany showed father-son incest to be 5 percent of all reported incest cases.[3]

Mother-daughter sexual contacts are fairly rare, but do occur. A four-year-old female was discovered to have primary syphilis, evidenced by a lesion on her vagina. The child had had repeated oral-genital contact with her mother, who was gay. The mother had apparently caught the disease from her female lover and passed it on to the child.[4]

Some therapists report an increase in cases of father-son and mother-daughter incest. It is rare, however, to find a case reported in the literature. "You think people are upset by incest," one therapist said. "These cases of same-sex incest really blow people's minds."

The Extent of the Problem

It is more difficult to come up with hard data on the occurrence of incest than with any other form of child sexual abuse. Because incest is so tightly cloaked within the family, incest is much less likely to be reported to police or social agencies. It is estimated that for every reported case of incest, at least twenty-five cases go undetected. Incest is not only underreported, it is also undertreated. For every five reported cases, no more than two receive any form of treatment.

Twenty years ago, most experts would have agreed that the incidence of incest was about one to two cases per million population.[5] That would mean about 200 to 400 cases a year in the United States. Recent experience, however, suggests that these figures are a gross underestimate of the actual occurrence of incest. In the early fifties, the Kinsey Report on female sexuality revealed that one out of sixteen white female women interviewed reported that they had been the object of an unwanted sexual contact by an adult relative when they were children. One-and-a-half percent reported that they had been molested by their fathers.

In 1976, Henry Giarretto, a man with considerable experience treating incestuous families as director of the Child Sexual Abuse Treatment Program in Santa Clara County, California, estimated that the one-in-a-million figure was at least 200 times too small. His rock-bottom estimate of 40,000 cases a year is probably still an underestimate. The figure may go as high as a quarter of a million cases a year.[6] The highest estimate that I have seen in the literature was that 20 million Americans may have been involved in incestuous experiences, a startling one in ten.[7]

Most experts agree that we are just beginning to scrape the surface of child sexual abuse and incest. Incest is probably not on the increase, but rather we are seeing the effects of better detection and reporting. Mandatory sex abuse reporting laws, child abuse hot lines, growing public and professional awareness of the problem, and a general easing of societal prohibitions against talking about the topic—all these have contributed to better detection.

It is not, as some people think, creating a problem where none existed before. Rather it is no longer pretending there is no problem when in reality there is a substantial one.

A Few Myths about Incest

There are many mistaken ideas about incest. One is that it is a phenomenon limited to Appalachia or other rural sections of the country. There is some truth to this, for in some places incest has been an accepted practice over many generations. However, incest is not limited to a few geographical areas nor to the lower socioeconomic classes. Social, economic, religious, ethnic, or geographical factors have very little to do with the incidence of incest. Nor is the rate of incest sensitive to a rise in population, population density, or fluctuations in the business cycle.[8] The only difference is that incest is more likely to come to the attention of the law when it involves the poor and uneducated.

Another myth is that the incest offender is psychotic. This is simply not true. Very few offenders are psychotic. Nor is it true that mother is unaware of what is going on. Most studies suggest that while the mother may not allow the fact of the incest into conscious awareness, she is most often aware of it on a preconscious level. This matter will be discussed further in chapter VI.

Another mistaken belief is that incest is a one- or two-time occurrence involving a single child in the family. Again, cases of incest emphatically refute this view. Incest cases have typically been going on for at least two years on the average prior to discovery. Sometimes they have gone undetected for five to ten years. Also, they are not confined to one child, but usually involve children sequentially by age in the family. Sometimes more than one child may be involved at the same time. Examples of children of both sexes being the objects of a father's attention are also known.

A view that is becoming more common these days, if one can believe the articles in semipornographic magazines, not to mention the frankly pornographic ones, is that incest is just another normal deviation in a varied sex life, a harmless way of adding spice to a jaded sex life.

Again, this is not true. Incest is an indication of family pathology and breakdown; it is symptomatic of emotional dysfunction in the family unit. While it is true that there may be little or no harmful *physical* effects to the child, incest rarely involving the use of force, the psychological effects are usually devastating. The major psychological difficulty can be traced to the violation by the adult of the child's trust. This point will be elaborated further in chapter VI.

Most authorities who write on incest devote considerable attention to the role of the incest taboo in society on the assumption that the taboo is effective in preventing incest. This is probably another myth. What is clear, however, is that the incest taboo plays a major role in preventing us from recognizing and treating both victims and offenders. By helping to keep incest in the dark, the taboo encourages the very behavior it is supposed to prevent.

Another myth that many would like to believe is that incest is less traumatic to the child victim than a sexual assault by a stranger. This is not true, as the following chapters will show. The psychological harm to a child when she or he is betrayed by a trusted adult cannot be overestimated.

Another myth is that a child born as the product of an incestuous relationship will be retarded or physically handicapped. While this sometimes happens, such a child can be entirely normal, both mentally and physically.

One final myth is that certain child victims of incest may be partially responsible for what happens to them because of their sexually seductive behavior toward an adult. This argument may arise in court cases where much emphasis is placed on it as a mitigating circumstance. (The same point is often made in the early literature on incest.) But there is no doubt that some children, especially if they live in sexually stimulating environments, can learn very seductive ways of relating. Regardless of how seductive or provocative the child may act, the ultimate responsibility for any sexual encounter between a child and an adult lies with the adult by virtue of greater age, experience, knowledge, understanding, supposed maturity, and the generally accepted social role of adults. The child simply does not have an adult's ability to make choices and decisions about sexual behavior.

The Victims

As is true with sexual abuse generally, 92 percent of the victims of incest are females, and 97 percent of the offenders are males. The median age of the first encounter is nine to eleven years. One study found that three fourths of the cases occurred before age twelve, and one fourth of those before age nine. The age of the victim can literally range from only a few months to the late teen-age years. Here are some examples of female victims:

A toddler is found to have gonorrhea of the mouth. She was infected by her father. In another case, a nine-month-old female has gonorrhea of the throat.

In Mineola, New York, Nassau County authorities break up a sex ring, which included policemen filmed having sex with their daughters. One child is three-and-a-half years old.[9]

A twelve-year-old physically abused child reports that her drunken father pinched her breasts and said, "You're doing it for other *boys*. You can do it with your father." She was able to evade his advances, but her younger sister was not as fortunate.[10]

A thirteen-year-old girl is raped by her stepfather, stepuncles, and then her stepaunt.[11]

A father rapes his sixteen-year-old daughter. Nine months later she gives birth to her own sister and her father's first grandchild.[12]

While female children bear the brunt of incest, boys, too, can be victims. Reported studies put the incidence of male victims at around 5 percent of all cases. Examples in the literature are rare, but here are a couple:

A teen-age boy is molested by his minister father. Shortly afterward, unable to cope with the situation, the boy hangs himself.[13]

One bizarre set of parents went into the pornographic photo business and used their nine-year-old son and his sisters as models. The children were photographed having sex with their father. When the boy became a teen-ager, his father brought men home who sodomized the boy and forced him to perform oral sex on them while the father recorded it on film.[14]

Mark, a nine-year-old boy in foster care, had been abused at home by a retarded uncle in his twenties. The uncle often stayed overnight at Mark's house, sharing a bed with one or more of the children. Mark's father was indifferent about the abuse. "Kids have to learn about that stuff sooner or later," he told the social worker. Mark's mother had a different reaction. She vehemently denied that Mark had been singled out. "He [the uncle] had sex with all the kids," the mother said.[15] (For a fuller discussion of this case, see Chapter XVI.)

There are indications that incest is no longer the "crime that nobody talks about." Many newspapers have carried articles about incest, including local resources for victims and their families. Features have appeared in slick magazines such as *Ms., Playgirl,* and *Redbook.* Even syndicated columnist Ann Landers has broached the topic. In the last half of 1977, I ran across four separate columns by her on the subject. The writers were women who either recounted their victimization as children or told of a current situation with their own children:

A widow who had remarried reported her discovery that the elder of her two daughters, sixteen years old, had been the object of sexual advances from her stepfather for two years.

A twelve-year-old child tried for over a year to explain to her mother her grandfather's advances, but she didn't have the language to describe the experiences clearly.

A woman reported that she was ten when her stepfather "bothered me." Another put it bluntly, "I was eleven when my stepfather raped me." Another told how her natural father had a sexual relationship with her for eight years.

This openness about incest is bound to have positive effects. Victims old enough to understand can learn that they are not unique in what is happening to them, that it does not have to continue, and that society will help protect them. Offenders, too, can know that society does not approve of what they are doing, but stands ready to help them with treatment services that will aim to preserve the family rather than to break it apart.

Chapter VI
Father-Daughter Incest

The fathers who are offenders in cases of incest are victims, too. Often, discovery brings shame, censure, loss of family, job, and perhaps prison. In an excellent article about incestuous fathers, Hector Cavallin makes the point that a review of the literature done in 1960 did not turn up a single case of an incestuous father who had been subjected to psychiatric examination and study.[1] Almost all of the psychiatric literature has been devoted to the daughters who are the victims. Cavallin's study is an attempt to redress that balance.

Cavallin studied twelve cases of incestuous fathers in Kansas and found the average age of the offenders at the time of the discovery of the incest to be just over thirty-nine years (the range was twenty to fifty-six years). The daughters averaged thirteen, with a range from three to eighteen years. In all cases but one, the relationship had lasted from a few months to a maximum of three years before detection.

The majority of fathers acknowledged the acts when confronted and pleaded guilty without a jury trial. Only two had a prior record of convictions and none had been in a psychiatric hospital. They were of average intelligence and had completed just over nine grades in school. Their work history was adequate.

All twelve of the men saw their wives as rejecting and threatening. In the men's own childhood history, the absence of at least one parent during infancy was noted. In three fourths of the cases, the mothers were absent because of death, abandonment, or working. The offenders came from large families, averaging 5.4 children.

Two of the fathers were psychotic, but they became so *after* the incest was reported. Three others were considered borderline psychotic. The rest were without obvious psychopathology. All, however, seemed prone to projection and paranoid thinking. Psychological testing suggested weak object relations, weak psychosexual identity, unconscious homosexual strivings, and projection as a major defense.

The composite picture that emerged included a sense of depression and inadequacy among the men. One felt as if he had lost his wife to the children. The marriage relationships were strained, with much arguing and tenseness. The men were uncomfortable with closeness to others. One man felt his wife and daughters had robbed him of his strength by forcing intercourse upon him and then deserting him. Another was blackmailed by his own daughter, who forced him to buy her secrecy about their sexual relationship and then to procure boys with whom she could have sex. This man felt himself to be the victim of both his wife and his daughter, who engaged in long, insulting tirades against him.

Most of the men in this study fell into the third of three types of incestuous fathers, the endogamic. These were men who confined their sexual objects to members of their own families. There is a strong emotional bond in these families, but it is a conflictive and pathological one. The other two types of incestuous fathers are those whose orientation is particularly toward young children, pedophilia, including their own daughters; and those who are indiscriminately promiscuous, where their incest is only a part of a general pattern of sexual psychopathology. In all three types, victims can be of either sex.

A third of the fathers in Cavallin's study drank to an excessive degree. Other authors indicate alcohol as playing a much greater role. At the Center for Rape Concern in Philadelphia, about half of the cases involve men who drink heavily and whose impulse control is severely weakened by alcoholism. While incest is certainly not caused by alcohol, there is little doubt that the incest taboo can be weakened by alcohol, as well as by other factors such as poverty, frustration, overcrowding, social isolation, divorce, rejection, desertion, and a poor marital situation. One must be cautious in interpreting the role of alcohol in incest. A favorite defense of offending fathers is, "I was drunk. I didn't know what I was doing." This may be a way of evading responsibility and blame. One must remember that alcohol in large doses generally inhibits sexual performance.

Other studies and clinical reports on the middle-class incestuous father show considerable agreement on a number of points. The average age is around thirty-five to forty. Usually these men are described as good providers and good husbands. Sometimes they are "pillars of the community." However, the men do seem to suffer from a poor self-image and may see themselves as failures in the work world. There is social isolation, with descriptions of the father's poor peer relationships. In spite of a cold and often rejecting wife, many of the men have an active sex life. They have high sexual demands and fear rejection by women.

The fear of rejection from adult women provides some insight into why such a man may turn to his daughters. He is usually confident that the child will not reject him. The daughter usually sees her father as "wonderful" and "great." She doesn't challenge or question him and is often initially flattered by the attention. This dynamic has been described as looking for the "youth connection." With the child's natural submission to the authority of the parent, the incestual situation is one in which the father can count on being in control.

The power element may play as important a part as any sexual motivation. The best summary of what went on in a father's mind when he turned to his daughter for sex was given by one father in response to his daughter's question, "Why did you do it to me?" The father's answer: "You were available and you were vulnerable."

The Dynamics of Incest

It is not an easy task to deal with the dynamics of incest. The focal point of any discussion should be on the family interactions since it has been stated that incest is a reflection of pathology in the family unit. It is the pattern of family psychodynamics that determines whether incest remains fantasy or becomes reality.

Incest begins when both father and daughter feel abandoned. Incest is really the story of a distorted search by each family member for caring and warmth. The predominant feelings that incestuous families have to cope with are the guilt, anger, and anxiety surrounding abandonment. In her book, *Betrayal of Innocence,* Susan Forward quotes a patient as saying: "We were all starved in my family—not for food, we always had plenty of money—but for feelings. Nobody ever seemed to feel anything. At least when I had sex with my father, I could feel something."

The prototype of the incestuous family is that of Lot and his daughters as recounted in Genesis. There was the ungiving and unavailable mother (who was turned into a pillar of salt). Since there were no available men to marry, Lot's daughters conspired to get him drunk and then slept with him. In this myth, too, alcohol is assigned a crucial role in the incest. Each in turn became pregnant by him and bore sons.

A word of caution to literal-minded readers. No parallel is intended between the scheming seduction by Lot's daughters and the modern-day situation. If anything, perhaps, the Bible story demonstrates the similarity of the psychic processes throughout history. For in this myth, as is often the case today, the reality of incest is denied, and the blame is shifted from the adult to the child. In a typical blame-the-victim maneuver, seduction becomes an act of the daughters who take advantage of their drunken father. Lot is the innocent victim who remains unaware that his daughters have slept with him.

The most famous perpetrator of the shift-the-blame game was the founder of psychoanalysis, Sigmund Freud. Early in his work, Freud was struck by how many of his female patients reported sexual encounters with their fathers. Unable to believe there were that many perverted fathers around, Freud instead concluded that there were more hysterical females than he had previously thought. He decided that his patients were not describing real events, but rather were revealing their fantasies from childhood. It wasn't that the fathers *did* anything, but rather that the daughters *wished* they had.

On the assumed fantasies of his patients and without directly seeing a single child in treatment, Freud constructed his theories of infantile sexuality and neurosis. In these theories he proposed that the underlying hysteria exhibited in his women patients was caused by Oedipal *fantasies* of seduction by the father. According to Freud his patients hadn't been seduced. The irony in this, of course, is that current experience is showing that sexual abuse of children by their fathers is much more common than anyone had thought. Amy Katan suggests that the childhood seduction of Freud's patients may have been factual, but they blamed the wrong person—their fathers. Six of her patients confused the perpetrator of a real childhood sexual assault with their fathers.[2]

A Family Scenario for Incest   We begin with a father, who as a child was denied access to a loving, warm mother.[3] Perhaps she was unavailable, or if present, cold and ungiving. He grows up with a sense of deprivation, poor self-esteem, and a smoldering hostility toward women. The father's background may have included poverty, alcoholism, inadequate housing, little education, and little parental warmth. He may have left home early to escape the unpleasant environment.

This man marries a woman unconsciously selected to be a duplicate of his mother. One sees in action the principle that childhood traumas which have never been mastered and resolved persist and play a role in recreating, in the present, the traumas of the past. The man, still infantile and dependent, expects to be mothered by his wife. She is incapable of meeting his demands and, perhaps under stress, becomes more like his mother—unavailable and ungiving. They argue and drift apart. He resents her more and more. Eventually there are children, and perhaps the father feels displaced and rejected by his wife.

Meanwhile, with her daughter, the mother may not be able to care and give. The child grows older, feels deprived by an unloving mother, is starved for nurturing, and resents her cruel, unjust, and depriving mother. The mother's social functioning suffers. Perhaps she turns to alcohol. She retreats further from her husband and daughter. The husband identifies his wife more with his mother, and displaces his hostility toward his mother onto the wife. In the face of this, she retreats even more and may withdraw from him sexually. One study of 100 incest cases found that 92 out of 100 mothers reported they were sexually unsatisfied. Further, 65 percent of these 92 mothers had had hysterectomies (the usual expectation would be 3 percent). To some, this suggests considerable dissatisfaction with the female role in these women.[4]

It is important to understand that the mother has her own problems in relating. As a child, she may have been sexually abused. It is not uncommon in incestuous families to find a history of sexual abuse as children in one or both of the parents as well as a history of parental desertion in both parents' families. The mother may be angry at men and increasingly fearful of her husband. She may have married a man with a propensity for violence. She may also be chronically depressed. The depression accounts for her inability to mother and her emotional distance from both her husband and daughter. The depression may also be related to her sexual withdrawal and passivity with her husband.

The mother's depression may be triggered by a physical incapacity such as illness, alcoholism, a hospitalization, or even entering the job market. At any rate, she all but abandons her role as mother and wife in the family. Sometimes of her own accord, the daughter may step in to fill mother's place to help keep the family intact. The mother may even encourage the daughter to take over her role in the family. In some cases, the assumption of a mother's role also means taking on her sexual role in meeting the father's needs. In this role reversal, the daughter plays the wife's role to her father and often maternal grandmother's role to her own mother. The father may see his daughter as a nurturing mother.

One study of the maternal grandmothers of incest victims showed them to be stern, demanding, controlling, cold, and extremely hostile women who rejected their daughters (the incest victim's mother) and pampered their sons.[5] The maternal grandfathers had deserted their families, and the maternal grandmothers selected one daughter whom they identified as being like the maternal grandfather and on whom they displaced their feelings of hurt and desertion.

When these daughters married, they married men who were dependent and infantile and who often deserted them in turn, a repetition of the pattern set by their fathers. They saw their marriages to these men as "throwing themselves away," thereby acting out their own mother's expectations of them, since she had rejected, destroyed, and thrown them away. These women are often tied to their mothers in a constant vain attempt to win love and approval and to ameliorate their poor opinion of themselves.

When the mothers married and had children, they also chose a special daughter whom they treated in a special fashion. They gave her excellent physical care, overindulged her, and encouraged her to assume responsibility beyond her years. Gradually this child is turned into a replica of the maternal grandmother. She becomes the mother's helper, adviser, confidante, and assistant mother. Then in a role reversal, the mother becomes the daughter again, and the daughter becomes the mother. Mother projects onto her daughter the hostility she originally felt for her own mother. She recreates the situation in which she is emotionally deserted by her husband and urges her daughter to take her place. When the incest event happens, these mothers typically show more hostility toward their daughters than toward their husbands. It is as though the daughters have become the bad part of themselves, the part that wanted to act out forbidden Oedipal feelings.

In short, everyone in the incestual family is searching for the mother they did not have. The basic anxiety of the family members revolves around abandonment by the mothering adult.

The stage is set. Both father and daughter feel abandoned, unloved and deprived. The father does not move in to take over the mother's role when she abdicates. He is more likely, instead of reaching out to care for the children, to sit back and expect the children to meet his needs. It is as though it is his right to continue to receive services—if not from his wife, then from his daughter. This may also include sexual rights. The actual incest may be triggered by a blow to the father's low self-esteem, such as the loss of his job.

Daughters of incestuous fathers see their mothers very negatively, but they are usually either ambivalent or positive toward their fathers. They may view him with warmth and turn to him to receive the affection they missed from their mothers. At the same time, they revenge themselves on the depriving mother by stealing her source of supplies. The child is looking for nurturing through sexuality. In search of caring and warmth, she finds instead physical closeness, petting, and perhaps intercourse.

At some level, the mother is aware of what is happening. It may be very open, as the mother who bluntly says to her daughter, "Tonight it is your turn to sleep with your father." Sometimes it is more subtle, as the mother who leaves her daughter sitting on the father's lap when she goes out and calls back over her shoulder to the girl as she leaves, "Now take good care of Daddy while I'm gone."

Because of the strain between herself and her mother, the child does not feel she can go to mother for support, protection, and help once the father begins sexual advances. Even those who try to tell their mothers are often met by indifference or disbelief. Inevitably, the daughter's angry feelings toward her mother increase. She feels betrayed, unsupported, and unprotected by her mother. Her rage over deprivation is further fueled by her anger that mother cannot or will not protect her from the father.

Sometimes the child senses that even if she were able to tell her story, mother in all probability would do nothing. The child may feel if her mother was forced to make a choice between her father and her, she would choose her father. She may well be right in that assessment. The mother's own problems are such that she is desperately afraid of being abandoned by her husband. A number of family histories of violence suggest that the mother may fear physical abuse from her husband. One mother told her daughter, "Some day you'll grow up and leave me, and then I'll only have Daddy for company. If I send him away, then I'll have nobody when I'm old."

When, and if, the daughter finally finds a way to tell her mother what has been happening, she hopes her mother will rescue her. Often the mother does nothing. She may take action such as bringing legal charges against her husband. However, when it becomes clear that the father may be taken from the family, she may withdraw the charges or force her daughter to withdraw her accusations. Faced with the choice between losing her husband and protecting her child, the mother chooses to keep her husband. She may turn against the child, calling her a liar and a slut and blaming her for seducing the father. The child learns the message quickly—she comes second. Mother will sacrifice her child to her husband.

Most of the daughter's anger at this state of affairs is reserved for the mother. Rarely do the child victims express anger toward the father for his behavior, even the sexual behavior itself. The child may continue to submit with resignation since she can do nothing to prevent the incest. Some may try to run away from home to avoid it.

Perhaps as many as half of these children will later admit that they experienced some degree of pleasure in the sexual contact. They suffer increased guilt for having enjoyed the contact and are even more confused about why it should have been pleasurable if it was wrong.

When an incest case does come to public attention, one of the common ways of dealing with the situation is to remove the child from the home and place her in foster care. This is an unfortunate solution. The child experiences this action as further confirmation that she has done something wrong since she is the one who is sent away. This adds to her already overburdened sense of guilt. The child feels her removal is further punishment for letting outsiders know what went on inside the house.

What is already an unhappy situation becomes infinitely worse when the child falls into the foster care network. It is very likely that the child will not be allowed to see her parents or visit home. She certainly will receive almost no psychiatric help. She runs the risk, if she stays in foster care more than a year, of becoming a professional foster child and never being returned to her parents. She becomes a double victim, first by her family and then by society. She learns not to trust adults and to see their expressions of caring as dangerous and harmful.[6]

The Effects of Incest

On a recent visit to a college campus, I saw a piece of graffiti painted on the railing of a bridge. Big yellow letters proclaimed, "Incest is best."

It is a myth that incest harms no one. There is little to suggest that incest is anything other than extremely hazardous to a child's mental
health. Less than a quarter of females involved in incestuous relationships escape with no apparent ill effects. In a clinical population of disturbed children, as many as 20 to 30 percent may have been involved
in incest.

It has already been stated that the key issue in incest, as far as
psychological damage goes, is the violation by the adult of the child's
trust. The father's sexual misuse of his daughter is clearly an abuse of
the social role of father, of power, and of parental authority over a
child. To make it worse, this offense occurs in the context of a supposedly caring relationship. It is this caring relationship that precludes
any need for force in most cases. The child is not raped but seduced
by the father. It is worse than an assault, it is a betrayal. The child
grows up distrusting adults and men in particular.

The child reacts by feeling helpless, powerless, and betrayed.
She senses she has been used, but is unable to express rage and anger
at her father. The anger goes underground and, following the time-
bomb principle, ticks away for years, often to erupt later on in a shattering explosion. The child victim may be in her forties before she
starts to deal with the delayed psychological effects of the incest experience.

One effect is that many child victims develop a strong hatred of all
men. Sometimes that hatred leads to actual revulsion. One child victim
summarized her attitude toward men succinctly: "All they want to do
is stick their pricks into little girls."[7]

Incest victims who have gone into therapy in later life reveal a
tremendous devaluation of themselves. They feel differently in some
way from other people, are socially isolated, and have trouble relating
to peers. They refer to themselves as witches, bitches, or whores. Some
expressed the devaluation as feelings of being dirty, unclean, or evil.
There was a nagging sense of guilt festering away, staining their image
of themselves. Some authors suggest that when an incest victim enters
adolescence, a depressive reaction associated with learning disabilities
and a regression to a preoccupation with unmet mother-child needs
are common. In general, depression and guilt seem to be reactions.

Further, in their relationships with men, these women in treatment
had considerable problems. Divorce, frigidity, failure to have orgasm,
and the inability to get close to men or trust them were common com-

plaints. Relationships with men were conflictual and often intensely masochistic. The women would let themselves be degraded and treated badly. As adults, a few women had also been raped and expressed the feeling that perhaps they had deserved it, another manifestation of unresolved guilt at work.

Some child victims grew up to feel that they had special powers over men. Having had sex with their fathers, they felt able to seduce any man. Behind this lay the fantasy that they had seduced their fathers. It is not surprising that some victims came to this conclusion. One has only to remember the helplessness and powerlessness they felt as children to prevent the incest. One common way children have of dealing with overwhelming trauma is to reverse the situation in fantasy. They become the powerful aggressor, the doer rather than the victim. Thus, "I was weak and was assaulted by my father" becomes "I seduced my father."

As the child grows older, this reversal in fantasy gets acted out in reality. The powerful seductive powers are put into operation, and the child-adult sleeps with men indiscriminately. Each time she goes to bed with a man, the constant denial and reaffirmation runs through her head. "It did not happen to me—I chose to do it to them." But the helpless terror is never stilled, the guilt never goes away, and she continues to sleep with every man in sight in the vain attempt to lay the ghosts in her head to rest. One day she will come to feel that she is the slut her mother called her, and the whore she calls herself.

Former incest victims who went into therapy also had conflictual relationships with women. These women were socially isolated from their peers and did not develop supportive and warm friendships with women. Some were plagued by the sense that they were bad, inadequate mothers like their own mothers had been. And some repeated their traumatic past by delivering up their own daughters to become new incest victims in a generational cycle of incest. They also were prone to marry men who sexually abused their daughters.

One of the unexpected effects of incest has been the alarming increase in venereal disease among children. Unlike what some adults imagine, people do not catch VD from toilet seats, door knobs, towels, or infected bedding. Children, like adults, catch VD from some form of sexual contact with an infected person. A child with VD should *always* raise the question in a professional's mind of the likelihood of sexual abuse.

Dr. Densen-Gerber, in a study of 118 women treated by Odyssey House programs (psychiatrically oriented residential therapeutic communities for the treatment of female drug abusers) in seven states, found that 44 percent of the women interviewed had been child victims of all types of incest. Nearly 65 percent of the incestuous partners of the women in this study (some had more than one partner) were cross-generational. Most common were uncles, cousins, in-laws, and quasi-family members, but 12 percent of all partners were natural fathers.[8]

Another study of 500 cases of adolescent drug abusers found 70 percent had been involved in some form of family sexual abuse.[9] A Minnesota study of adolescent female prostitutes revealed that 75 percent had been victims of incest.[10] It is also estimated that nearly one half of the 300,000 annual runaways in this country were sexually abused. In the Densen-Gerber study mentioned above, 52 percent of the incest group had left home by sixteen years of age, as compared to only 39 percent of a nonincest group.

These and other studies suggest quite strongly that incestuous behavior leads directly or indirectly to serious crimes, juvenile delinquency, drug abuse, and/or sexual promiscuity.

To sum up, one sees two common effects of incest. In one, there is a suppression of feeling, leading to coldness, avoidance of sex, withdrawal from people, and difficulties relating to men. In the other, the original feelings of helplessness and rage that were aroused in the victim of incest are suppressed. This leads to acting out sexually and deviant antisocial behavior. These two effects are not always mutually exclusive.

There is some suggestion that the child victim sees the incest as a way of saving the family. She takes the guilt upon herself and endures the behavior in an effort to keep her parents together. When the relationship is discovered, the child's guilt may center more strongly around her failure to keep the family from breaking up than on the violation of the incest taboo itself.

Other phase specific (but not trauma specific) reactions to incest are: feeding and sleep disturbances, learning difficulties, somatic complaints (abdominal pain is common, probably related to pregnancy fantasies), anxiety, hyperactivity, withdrawn behavior, fatigue, and generalized aches and pains.

From psychological testing on one group of eleven incest victims, the following picture of the girls emerged. The Rorschach revealed depression, anxiety, confusion over sexual identification, fear of sexuality, oral deprivation, and oral sadism. The Thematic Apperception Test (TAT) revealed that these girls depicted their mothers as cruel, unjust, and depriving. The children were more ambivalent in describing their fathers, some seeing them as nurturant, sometimes as weak and ineffectual, and sometimes as frightening. Other tests confirmed the sexual identity confusions of the children.[11]

Incest may also create problems for the female siblings of an incest victim. One study of the "unchosen" ones showed that these girls felt worthless, rejected, and discarded by their fathers because another sister was selected instead.[12]

The eventual outcome of sexual involvement depends upon the child's level of ego development, the quality of the parent-child interaction, the nature of the event, the adult involved, whether the sexual involvement was an isolated event or part of a continuing experience, and how supportive the child's mother is.

The outcome will also depend upon diverse factors external to the family itself, such as whether society's reaction is punitive or supportive, whether the family is broken up, whether the child is placed in foster care or remains at home, whether the child receives treatment, whether the child is scapegoated by peers or other family members and relatives, or whether the child is exposed to a criminal trial and the nature of the courtroom experience. Any professional who tries to help a child victim of incest must pay careful attention to the impact of all of these factors in order to give the most effective assistance.

Chapter VII
The Treatment of
Father-Daughter Incest

In spite of the known harmful consequences of incest, there are few treatment resources available to help child victims deal with the trauma. Professionals need special training to aid incest victims, and few if any have it. (Some experts believe that male therapists can be of little help to a female victim, largely because of their tendency to identify with the aggressor and their limited ability to appreciate the situation from the victim's viewpoint.) However, assuming a professional is competent to engage in some recognized form of psychotherapy, the additional training necessary to aid incest victims is largely a matter of education about incest and developing appropriate attitudes toward the incest victim and her family.

For example, the professional needs to know about the many myths of incest that will interfere with understanding the problem. She or he also needs to know that incest is much more common than recognized. In those cases in which the client voluntarily reveals an incestual episode, the professional must learn to accept the client's story at face value. Nothing is more destructive to therapeutic rapport than to treat the client's revelation as a mere fantasy. As a matter of fact, studies of reported cases of incest have shown that very few of them are actually false reports. Even in the case of adolescents, where the assumption is often made that a report is "hysterical," the chances are that the report is true. It is better to err on the side of believing the report than to shut off what may be a client's cry for help.

The tendency to assume that a child who reports incest is "making it up," is fortunately becoming less frequent as health professionals, the police, and the general public become more informed about the realities of incest. One heartening example of this came to light recently in a suburban community. An eleven-year-old girl was picked up by the police as a runaway. At the police station she told the officers a horrendous tale of incest involving oral and anal activities that she had been subjected to over the past five years. Her story was taken seriously, and upon investigation her four siblings confirmed the basic facts. Confronted with this, the father confessed. The remarkable thing about this case was that the child involved was seriously emotionally disturbed, perhaps psychotic! In spite of her peculiar affect and occasional wild flights of fantasy, her story was believed by the police. Even in the case of an obviously psychotic child, the professional would do well to assume incest to be a fact until proven otherwise.

Professionals, like everyone else, harbor a basic horror of incest. In order to work sympathetically with incest victims and their families, they need to bring those feelings under control and replace them with a professional detachment coupled with sensitivity. They need also to appreciate the realities of what the discovery of incest can mean to a family—in terms of possible prison sentence for the offender, loss of income to the family, or the splitting apart of the family. They need to know the realities of foster care as a "solution" and its impact on the child victim. The professional must also be well grounded in the psychological aftereffects of incest on the child victim.

There are also many practical issues the professional needs to know in order to deal adequately with incest cases. For example, it is often assumed that once the incest becomes publicly known, the danger to the child is past. One cannot afford to be complacent after incest becomes known. There are fathers who have resumed the incest after the initial furor has died down, as well as those who resumed their activities after serving a prison sentence. Not even removal of the child victim from the home ends the problem. If there are younger female siblings at home, they become at risk when the original victim is removed.

Any professional who works with incest families should be prepared for the possibility that the family members may refuse to cooperate. Even the original victim may do an about-face and retract her story. One should expect this and continue efforts to help the family. The sudden change of family attitude is indicative of the tremendous stresses that uncovering the incest has put on all of the family members, and of their fears for the survival of the family. The resistance to treatment, particularly that of the offender, is one reason why the involvement of the legal system in requiring treatment is often helpful.

Ideally, the treatment of incest would involve a trained crisis-intervention team and close cooperative efforts between all of the professionals involved—police, courts, probation officers, mental health professionals, social workers, and others. However, the response of the courts and the law to incest victims is usually inadequate. The emphasis is most often on punishment and prison sentences for the offender, thus breaking the family apart and throwing an already devastated mother and child into financial stress. Sometimes the child victim is placed in foster care. Little is done to reconstitute the family; treatment is almost never prescribed.

About the only ray of light on an otherwise dismal treatment scene, is the model Child Sexual Abuse Treatment Program (CSATP) of Santa Clara County, California.[1] This program began in 1971 under its director, Henry Giarretto. It is basically a treatment program lasting from six months to a year, utilizing individual therapy, conjoint family therapy, and self-help and support groups.

Because the incestuous family is so badly fragmented—first by the original family dysfunction, and secondly by the disclosure of the incest to the civil authorities—it is impossible to begin treatment with family therapy. Instead, the program calls for individual sessions for the child, mother, and father. Next, mother and daughter are counseled together. An aim of this interaction is for the mother to admit to the child that she (mother) had been unable to parent her daughter adequately. The next step is marital counseling, a must if the family wishes to be united. At this point, mother begins to realize that her husband was not such a bad provider and father, and that the family misses and needs him.

Father-daughter counseling is the next step. Here the important goal is for the father to admit to his daughter that the incest was wholly his fault, and that she does not share the blame or the guilt for what happened. This is not easy for the father, but it is an essential step if the treatment is to be successful.

The next step is family counseling, and this leads into the last phase—group counseling. The group counseling aspect of the program has led to the formation of a self-help and support group for parents known as Parents United. A similar group, Daughters United, is available to the child.

The parents' group has many options available. After meeting together for eight weeks in an orientation group, the parents are then transferred to another group. It might be an intense couples group, limited to six couples; a father's group; a mother's and daughter's group; or a mixed group for those not currently living with a sexual partner. The support the parents get in knowing that they are not unique or alone in their problem is invaluable. So, too, is seeing other couples who have made progress and reunited their families.

Giarretto's program meets under the auspices of the Juvenile Probation Department. Giarretto has worked closely with the police, probation officers and the courts. As a result, offenders in Santa Clara County are given either suspended or shorter sentences. While Giarretto believes the law alone is not sufficient to bring about changes (and neither is therapy), he insists that the courts are valuable in the treatment by keeping pressure and motivation on the father to stay in treatment. The law also has other advantages, he feels, among them giving the offender a chance to satisfy an expiatory factor. The offender needs to know in no uncertain terms that what he did was wrong, that the community will not stand for incestuous behavior, and that it will exact a punishment.

In the six years since the program began, over 600 families have received a minimum of at least ten hours of treatment. Ninety percent of the children involved have been returned to their families within a month, and an additional 5 percent have eventually been returned. About 90 percent of the marriages have been saved. To date, there has been no recidivism among the families treated.

The increased awareness of the program by public and judiciary, and the growing confidence in it, is a mixed blessing. When the program opened in 1971, 35 cases were referred for treatment. In 1975, the number had risen to 180. In the first quarter of 1976, 102 referrals were received! At present, referrals run 600 a year.

The program has become a model for a demonstration center established in 1976 by the California Legislature. The program has also received nationwide attention. The CSATP staff have filled requests for hundreds of informational packets from people all over the country. Training sessions for professionals are also part of the program to help spread the CSATP's success to other areas.

The program is based on the tenets of humanistic psychology. A basic premise is that when parents don't feel good about themselves, they develop a self-hatred that can only be discharged by acts of abuse toward themselves and others. Child neglect, abuse, battering, and sexual abuse results. The program aims to help parents and children feel good about themselves and to learn how to nurture each other.

The specific attitudes dealt with are: Mother must say to the child, "You are not to blame. Daddy and I had a bad marriage. That is why Daddy turned to you." Father must admit and believe that his behavior was wrong and cannot be repeated. He must tell the daughter the responsibility was his, and apologize to the daughter for his behavior. At the same time, the father must be assured that the family will be helped and worked with, not destroyed. Attempts are made to develop the father's capacity for gentleness and tenderness, and to channel these feelings toward his wife. The mother is helped to see the child not as a rival, but as an innocent bystander.

Giarretto believes any community can start its own incest treatment program. He believes society's attitudes toward incest are so punitive that if any treatment program is to succeed, it must combine hard-nosed practicality with compassion. The CSATP exists to help provide a humane alternative to family dismemberment and incarceration. It does not help offenders evade punishment and responsibility for their actions, but allows them to find help and rehabilitation instead.

Chapter VIII
Other Types of Incest

The bulk of Part II has concentrated on father-daughter incest. According to Masters and Johnson, the type of incest that professionals encounter most often is that between brother and sister.[1] Some experts feel this type of incest is five times more common than father-daughter incest, although it is certainly reported much less often.

Brother-Sister Incest

In Masters and Johnson's opinion, brother-sister incest is the least damaging in its effects on the participants. This is because it is usually transitory and often takes the form of experimentation between young teen-agers. They report one case of a woman who, at age thirteen, began incestual relations with her two brothers, fourteen and sixteen. This went on for nearly three years. The brothers made her available to their friends, and it was this sexual behavior that caused her problems, rather than the incest.

In the absence of this type of exploitation, incest with an older brother is usually not the root cause of later sexual problems in the sister. Of potentially more harm is the seduction of a young teen-age boy by an older sister. Two cases are reported by Masters and Johnson and both male victims, when they became young adults, had a problem with impotence. This kind of relationship often involves a semimaternal aspect where the older sister behaves in a motherly way.

In general, society is fairly tolerant of sexual contact between siblings, especially if it is of short duration and exploratory in nature. There may be some concern if there is a wide age difference between the sibs, if the contact is forced, or if pregnancy, infection, or trauma result. For children more or less the same age, even if of the same sex, sexual behavior of an incestuous nature is not usually that upsetting to the family if discovered. The motto of "Kids will be kids," seems to prevail.

Brother-Brother Incest

Like brother-sister incest, virtually nothing has been written on the topic of brother-brother incest. A great deal of this type of sexual contact goes on, but it is largely transient, curiosity, or sex-play behavior. Presumably, brother-brother incest is not abuse or misuse unless there is a considerable age difference between the two partners, unless it continues over an extended period of time, or unless it lasts well into adolescence to the exclusion of the development of heterosexual relationships. A fictionalized account of such a relationship between twin brothers can be found in the recent best-seller, *Twins* by B. Wood and J. Geasland.

The only other account I have seen of brother-brother incest was a pornographic book which purported to be a scientific study. (Before the liberalization of sexual attitudes, a good deal of pornography tried to pass itself off as a scientific study of sexual behavior.) The book's pornographic purpose was obvious in its detailed and sensationalized descriptions of the sexual behaviors of the "brothers" along with the graphic color photographs. The book might seemingly appeal to homosexuals, with the incest theme perhaps adding additional spice.

In my personal practice, I have seen only one such case involving a ten-year-old boy and his fifteen-year-old brother. The victim was showing near psychotic behavior when I first saw him. However, when he was able to reveal his secret and discuss his sexual behavior, the symptoms disappeared. Alerting his parents to what was going on enabled them to effectively protect the boy from his brother.

Mother-Son Incest

Masters and Johnson state that the most traumatic form of incest is mother-son contact. The boy's social relationships with peers of both sexes are badly damaged. The authors set forth two types of mother-son incest, neither one of which actually involves intercourse. Both types basically involve a father who is absent from the home, through death, divorce, or desertion.

In the first type, there is early seduction in the mothering relationship, commonly in bathing routines. Eventually this leads to masturbatory stimulation of the very young child by the mother. By puberty the pattern is firmly established in which she brings him to ejaculation manually.

The second pattern involves the young boy replacing the father in his mother's bed. While no intercourse takes place, there is much physical closeness, exposure, nudity, manipulation, and fondling. The overstimulated child has sex dreams of his mother, reinforced in puberty by nocturnal emissions. In effect, the incest has become an emotional reality for the child even without direct genital contact.

An article by C. W. Wahl presents two cases of mother-son contact.[2] Both involved men in their late twenties who had recently had intercourse with their mothers. Both men had a history of hospitalization for schizophrenia. Both men had been deprived of their fathers as children, one when he was four-and-a-half years of age and the other when he was seven. Both men suffered from fears that they might be homosexual. One mother used this fear to initiate sexual intercourse with her son by suggesting that he would become homosexual unless she gave him some "special training," i.e., had sex with him. The author of the article speculates on the importance of incestual wishes as a stressor and precursor in the genesis of schizophrenia. However, one should not take these speculations too seriously.

Father-Son Incest

While the dynamics of father-daughter incest have been well elaborated in the literature, no such formulation has been put forth for any type of homosexual incest. Father-son incest was estimated in one study to comprise only 5 percent of all cases of reported incest. It is rare to find a case of father-son incest reported in the literature. A study of a single case in 1976 reported finding only two other case reports in the literature up until that time.[3]

In all three cases it was felt that the fathers were either overt or latent homosexuals. This was not just because of their involvement with their sons, but because of the fathers' prior histories of homosexual contacts. There did not seem to be any particular family stress situations at the time of the episodes with the sons. It was suggested that the father's intrapsychic conflicts played a more important role in father-son incest than in father-daughter incest. Other writers suggest the physical/emotional unavailability of the father may contribute to a child's engaging in homosexual incest with a relative or a sibling.

Because the father-son incest cases reported in the literature are barely more than anecdotes, there is very little understanding of the dynamics of the situation, the traumatic effects, or the nature of treatment. In essence, it is a very neglected area. In the opinion of some experts, homosexual incest will become more common as the previously hidden phenomenon of incest is brought to light. Rossman estimates that of the 1 million American men over twenty-one who have had sex contacts with teen-age boys, at least 10 percent were incestuous. If one includes cousins, uncles, brothers, and other relatives, the figure for those who seduce their own family members may be as high as 30 percent.[4]

Mother-Daughter Incest

This kind of incest is also a relatively unknown area. Again, only scant anecdotal material exists.

A thirty-nine-year-old housewife, mother of five children, was hospitalized for depression when an extended homosexual affair came to an end. During treatment she admitted to an intense homosexual interaction with her mother when she was twenty-six years of age. The woman had been separated from her mother in infancy and placed in a foster home. Reunited many years later, the two lived together for awhile, during a time when both mother and daughter were separated from their respective husbands. It was during this time that the mother initiated the homosexual relationship.[5]

In my own clinical experience, I have run across only one case of mother-daughter incest. The mother was divorced and living an active lesbian life-style. Her five-year-old daughter apparently witnessed love-making between her mother and an adult female partner. In between her adult partners, the mother turned to her daughter for sexual satisfaction. By eight years of age, the child showed marked anxiety, preoccupation with sexual ideas, frequent sex talk, and numerous attempts to initiate sexual behavior with other girls her age.

Because mother-daughter incest is such an unstudied area, very little can be said about either its frequency of occurrence or any potential disruptive aftereffects.

Mothers and Sexual Abuse

One of the interesting facts that few pay any attention to is that mothers rarely abuse their children sexually. There are a couple of viewpoints as to why this should be so.

One view is that sexual assaults on children are often expressions of anger, hostility, power, and dominance. Women in our society are not used to expressing anger/power in direct forms. They keep a tight rein on their anger and express it in subtle ways. On the whole, all forms of violent crimes by women are fairly rare. Most violence is done by men, trained to be competitive, aggressive, dominant, and to strike out at frustrations in their environment.

J. Herman and L. Hirschman, in a journal article on father-daughter incest, present an intriguing feminist viewpoint on this matter.[6] They draw the generalization that the greater the degree of male supremacy in any culture, the greater the likelihood of father-daughter incest. (Mother-son incest, on the other hand, is an affront to the father's prerogatives.) The authors argue that the incest taboo is created and enforced by men and is essentially an agreement regarding sexual access to women. Because the taboo is a male creation, they believe it is more easily and frequently violated by men. They point out that little boys learn a different version of the taboo than little girls.

In the classical Freudian Oedipal situation, the little boy learns that his sexual desires for his mother can never be consummated because his mother belongs to his father. The father reinforces his ownership by virtue of the fact that he has the power to punish the son for violations of the taboo. The threat of castration impels the boy to renounce any claim on his mother and to look outside of the family for his woman. He contents himself with the knowledge that when he becomes a man he will be able to possess a woman of his own.

If the boy marries and has a daughter, the taboo against sexual contact with the daughter will not carry the same force as the one that prohibited incest with his mother. Very simply: there is no punishing father to avenge father-daughter incest.

The situation for a little girl is very different. She learns that she is weak and powerless as a child and will remain so as a woman—like her mother. The only way for her to acquire strength is through attachment to a powerful man. She has little incentive, then, to resolve her Oedipal complex toward her father. The threat of castration carries no fear for her. If a girl wants to commit incest, she marries a man like her father.

This is an intriguing attempt to solve a puzzling fact—why women so rarely abuse children sexually. To women already used to exchanging sexual services for care and protection, the taboo is just another aspect of their submission to men. Women understand better what happens when one introduces sex into a relationship where power is so unequally distributed. Perhaps they also understand better the difference between affection and erotic contact, and the appropriate limits of parental love.

At a recent conference on sexual abuse, physician Susan Sgroi reported that in all her experience with sexual abuse cases, she had only seen three cases of mother-child sexual abuse. In two of these cases, the mother was psychotic, and, in the other, she was retarded.[7] This would seem to suggest that women violate the incest taboo only when their judgment is impaired by mental illness or retardation. It is ironic that the psychotic father offender turns out to be a myth, but from the very little information available about mothers as offenders, psychosis may be an important part of their committing a sex offense. Altogether, incest is a radically different psychological event for female offenders than for males.

PART III
Sexual Misuse of Male Children

Chapter IX
Neglected Victims

It comes as a surprise to many to find that men and boys are raped, too, or that males are incest victims. Statistical reports in the literature suggest that the sexual abuse of males is not very common—about 5 percent of all child victims. However, in almost all cases, the offenders are other males. Hence the public is likely to believe that male children are seldom sexually misused, and when they are, that the offender is a homosexual male.

These conclusions, of course, are wrong on both counts. The ratio of male to female victims more closely approximates 1:2 and may even be equal. A study by the San Francisco Police Department's Youth Services Division during 1975-1976 revealed that of a total of 131 identified juvenile victims of sex offenses, nearly one-third were males.[1] A study of college students in the Northeast found that about one third of both male and female students reported an unwanted sexual contact with an adult in childhood.[2]

As for the offenders, studies suggest that these men are much more likely to have a heterosexual history and orientation than a homosexual one. Contrary to public belief, homosexual adult males rarely molest young male children.

In a survey of men imprisoned for homosexual offenses, 40 percent of whom had a previous conviction for a nonsexual crime, a quarter of those sentenced for offenses with young boys also had committed offenses with young girls. Less than a quarter of them were exclusively attracted to young boys. A large study by the Indiana University Institute for Sex Research showed that only 9 percent of men convicted for homosexual offenses with adults had ever had contact with children, and only one percent admitted to a preference for children.[3]

The sexual misuse of male children is a poorly understood area of child abuse, replete with much misinformation and many myths. In all probability the dynamics of sexual misuse of males have little in common with those involving females. Society reacts much differently to a male child who is molested than to a female child. The attitude still prevails that females are helpless and need to be protected. "Society is made to take care of little girls, not boys," a police officer said. "You don't tell boys not to take candy from a stranger."[4]

When a female child is sexually attacked, the reaction of the father is rage—partly because someone has damaged his property. To attack a man's daughter is to attack his prized possession. The sexuality of female children is carefully guarded, for little girls grow up to be mothers and to serve their husband's sexual needs.

A major concern when a female child is attacked is that the experience will turn her off to men and to sex. The experience is seen as traumatic and potentially damaging to the child's sexual and emotional development. Damaged goods must be restored to their prerape value.

Reporting the rape of a female child is embarrassing, for among other things, it exposes a father's inability to protect his daughter. But the desire for vengeance is stronger than with male children, and many cases are reported.

When a male child is sexually attacked, however, the picture is different. First, we expect males to learn how to take care of themselves. They are expected to "tough it out" and shoulder their own problems. The idea of help for an attacked male child is likely to consist of "Stop crying and forget it."

There is another subtle difference involved here, too. While in the case of the female victim, the father experiences rage because his property has been violated, in the case of the male victim, the father does not interpret the incident as a personal insult, but rather grieves for the damage done to his son's masculinity. Admitting to the rape of his son is far more humiliating for a father than to admit to the rape of his daughter. One father said to the doctors in the emergency room following a sexual attack on his son, "They've taken away my son's masculinity."

Note another curious difference. The concern of adults is that the female victim will be repulsed by sex after the attack, for it was assumed to be unpleasant for her. But in the case of the male, the fear is that having lost his masculinity, the child will become a homosexual,

as if the experience had been pleasant for the boy. Heterosexual rape
of a female child will turn her against men and sex, but homosexual
rape of a male child will turn the boy toward men and homosexuality.

Involved here is a cultural phenomenon, the American male's
excessive dread of anything that smacks of homosexuality. Homophobia in American males has been thoroughly discussed by many
writers. Ever since Freud introduced the idea that fear often covers
up a suppressed wish, homophobia has been seen as a defense against
underlying homosexual wishes and fantasies.

The reaction to the rape of the male child is a case in point. Why
shouldn't the child be disgusted and revolted by his experience, and
turned off to sex with men? The unconscious expectation of the adult
male is that the male child actually enjoyed the experience. Homosexuality is so contagious that if you are exposed to it, you become
one. In fact, you only have to listen to what one teaches, and you
become a convert. This is the basic tenet of homophobia, the fear that
if you try it, you'll like it. One homosexual contact supposedly de-
stroys a boy's masculinity.

With a female child, there is little direct evidence of whether or not
she "enjoyed" it. If she was penetrated, it is easy to assume that this
was against her will. It is different with a male child. Let the offender
state that the boy had an erection during the assault, and everyone
jumps to the conclusion that he must have enjoyed it. Regardless of
the fact that it feels good to have the penis touched, and this triggers
off a physiological reaction, an erection in a male victim is seen as
evidence that he must have been consenting. In fact, the presence of
an erection is evidence that the child was not fearful or under duress.

Are Attacks on Male Children Homosexual Assaults?

The answer to that question depends greatly upon how one defines
homosexuality. If defined as any sexual contact between two people
of the same sex, then the answer to the above question is "yes." But
that is not what we usually mean by homosexuality. The usual definition of a homosexual is someone whose sexual partners are limited
almost exclusively to persons of his own sex. Using that definition,
then, most attacks on male children are not committed by homosexuals, but by men whose primary sexual orientation is heterosexual!

One study that throws light on this question is the one by Groth and Birnbaum.[5] As one remembers from Chapter IV, Groth divided 175 males convicted of sexual offenses against children into two classes of offenders, the regressed offender and the fixated offender. Of Groth's ninety-two regressed offenders, only fifteen chose male victims and an additional twelve chose both male and female victims. The other sixty-five men chose female victims exclusively. Of the twenty-seven men involved with males, eight had an exclusively heterosexual adult sexual orientation. Of these eight, five chose boy victims, and three chose both boy and girl victims. The remaining nineteen had a bisexual adult orientation, which meant they engaged in sex upon occasion with both men and women. (In no case did this attraction to men *exceed* their preference for women. Groth did not find a single case of a peer-oriented homosexual male who regressed to children.) Of these nineteen regressed offenders, ten chose male victims exclusively, and nine both male and female. Three other regressed offenders were also adult bisexuals, but chose only female victims.

The fixated offenders were different in that they chose male victims over female victims (males were 43 percent, females 34 percent, and both sexes, 24 percent). By definition these men had not achieved an adult sexual orientation since their interest was exclusively in children as sexual partners. Some of these men were probably homosexual pedophiles who exclusively chose boys. They tended to be uninterested in *adult* homosexual contacts and frequently expressed a strong sexual aversion to adult males, often labeling adult homosexuality as "unnatural."

Adult homosexuals are often attracted to masculine qualities in their partners. Yet these homosexual pedophiles found the "feminine" qualities of the boys appealing. They chose prepubescent boys (average age eleven years) who were soft, lacked body hair, and whose bodies were rounded rather than angular and muscular. The homosexual pedophile often focused on the rear of the child, from which view both sexes look similar, that is, feminine.

Groth concluded that the regressed offender is heterosexual in his adult orientation, and that homosexual pedophilia is not synonymous with homosexuality. In all his clinical experience he has never seen a regressed homosexual offender.

By contrast, the recent extensive study of homosexuals in San Francisco by the Kinsey research group reported that one fourth of the homosexuals studied admitted that they had had one or more sexual contacts with children under sixteen years of age.[6]

Still, the conclusion seems justified that the adult heterosexual male constitutes a greater risk sexually to underage children than does the adult homosexual male.

A Profile of Victims and Offenders

The popular stereotype of the man who has sex with boys is that he is middle-aged and unmarried. In fact, far more common is the middle-aged, married man with children of his own and a wife with whom he has regular sexual intercourse.

The Los Angeles Police Department compiled a profile of the man who uses boys.[7] He is described as married, often financially secure, often holds a college degree, has poor interpersonal relationships with adults, acts considerate of his victims, usually is nonviolent, passive, takes pride in his personal cleanliness, often works with youth services, likes children, may associate with other "boy lovers," is often considered a "good" citizen, generally takes pictures of his victims which he swaps with his pals, and prefers his boys as young as possible (down to ten to twelve years).

The LAPD also described the boy victims as usually eight to seventeen years of age, underachievers in school or at home, usually no previous homosexual activity or record of delinquency, underdeveloped physically with no secondary sex characteristics, from a low-income background in the West and East coast areas and an average background in the Midwest, having parents who are often absent either physically or psychologically from the home, having no strong moral or religious affiliations (in either family or boy), and exhibiting poor sociological development but a warm personality.

With these traits in mind, let's take a closer look at sexual misuse of males.

Chapter X
Pederasty—Contacts
with Teen-age Males

One area of concern about sex with male children involves the adult male with an interest in teen-age boys—that is, boys from twelve to sixteen years of age. The best description of this sexual subculture is obtained from Parker Rossman's book, *Sexual Experience between Men and Boys: Exploring the Pederast Underground.*[1] The term *pederast,* as used by Rossman, means a male over eighteen years of age who is sexually attracted to and involved with boys between the ages of twelve and sixteen. His definition is used here and should be kept in mind, for pederast, like many words in this area, has different meanings. It is sometimes used to mean a man who has anal intercourse with boys. Another usage refers to a male with a sexual interest in boys, regardless of the child's age. Rossman's term is restricted to sex with boys twelve to sixteen years of age.

The pederast is usually distinguished from the gay homosexual. The pederast is not, strictly speaking, homosexual. There are gay homosexual pederasts, but they usually are involved with teen-age boys whose sexual orientation is already homosexual. The pederast prefers heterosexually oriented males and the sex-for-fun horseplay of the normal masculine boy. The pederast himself is usually either bisexual or otherwise heterosexual for much of his life. The pederast tends to avoid gay homosexual teen-agers, largely because these relationships can become intensely erotic, love relationships, with the boy often extremely jealous and possessive of his sexual partner.

The difference between a pederast relationship and a homosexual one is that the gay homosexual orientation is more of a life-style where sex is part of a quest for love. By contrast, the pederast orientation is more incidental than a life-style. Sex is on a recreational basis, playful in nature. There is a quality of masculine horseplay, a couple of men getting together to play with each other. There is no attempt on the part of the pederast to feminize the boy sex object, nor for either of the two participants to play a feminine role.

Rossman estimates that at least one million American men over twenty-one have been involved in one or more sex acts with teen-age boys. Another half-million men value sex play with boys and believe it should not be against the law. Another 2 million men may have had deviant and illegal sex acts with boys under sixteen while segregated from women (in prison, for example), as tourists (especially in Turkey and Northern Africa), or as servicemen overseas (in Vietnam, Korea, and the Orient). There are many cultures where the sexual union between men and boys is looked upon with favor.

Some experts believe a suppressed sexual attraction toward boys is a common part of most male psyches, though the majority of men strongly suppress this awareness. Rossman estimates—and that's all it can be—that over 10 million American men have at one time or another been consciously aware of being erotically attracted to, and sexually tempted by, a teen-age boy. Some observers suggest that much of the emotional antigay, anti-sex-for-pleasure emotions in Western society are rooted in every man's suppressed pederast desires. Others suggest that because men are so powerless to deal with their own sexual desires in healthy and constructive ways, they are unable to intelligently handle pederast activity in others. Instead they react in emotionally negative ways.

One study suggests that three fourths of pederasts were aware of their sexual interest in young boys by the time they were eighteen. Almost two thirds of them had been sexually involved with a younger boy during their teen-age years. Only 8 percent had their first sexual contact with a boy after the age of thirty.

The last fact is of importance to the myth that boys are seduced into homosexual behavior by sexual contacts with older men. Actually, a boy's first sexual contact with another male is likely to be with an adolescent boy rather than with a man. The experience is often quite pleasant and can lead to other contacts with males. For such a boy himself to become a pederast when older, however, there has to be a further psychic determinant.

What that determinant may be is not at all clear. Some experts think boys who do become homosexual or pederasts are preconditioned by earlier childhood experiences. Others believe that something happens to the potential pederast's heterosexual ability somewhere between the twelfth and fifteenth year of his life. This view is supported by the finding that imprisoned pederasts (as opposed to other types of offenders) show a striking decline in the percentage of heterosexual activity at about age fifteen.

Another theory revolves around the sexual fantasy life, masturbation, and the childhood sex play, of the developing adolescent boy. Again, imprisoned pederasts showed the highest percentage of masturbation before puberty (57 percent) and the largest percentage of prepubertal sex play (84 percent) of all the sex offender groups in prisons. (Generalizing from imprisoned pederasts may be a dubious procedure. Rossman found in the over 1000 pederasts he interviewed that only 1 percent of practicing pederasts had ever been arrested. Of these, less than 3 percent of the men guilty of an indictable pederast offense ever go to prison.)

Obviously, early sex play and masturbation alone don't turn a boy into a homosexual or a pederast. This is where the role of fantasy comes in. It may be that the fantasies accompanying these sexual acts become addictive and function as a substitute for coitus. Fantasy sometimes serves as a substitute for actual sex (some pederasts try to use pornography as a substitute for sex contact with boys), and at other times, it may be the trigger to initiate sexual contact.

The late educator Paul Goodman, an acknowledged pederast, said, "If you wish to understand any pederast, or the sexual experience of any human being, explore his dreams. Only in that rich world of fantasy and concealed experience is the truth about ourselves in any way revealed."

Not having sex experiences with other males may allow the fantasy to assume unusual strength and importance. Considerable spice and excitement is added to the idea of what an actual sexual contact might be like. Behavior modification has shown that deviant sexual acts and fantasies can be reinforced by the orgasm. Thus, a boy masturbating to fantasies of sexual encounters with other boys or men receives powerful reinforcement for these fantasies when he climaxes. This may be enough to lead some boys eventually into real-life experimentation with sex with men.

Because pederast activity is illegal and driven underground, and because it is so rarely reported in the professional literature, there is

little chance to study it. Consequently, the understanding of pederasty
—its origins and dynamics—is very poor. It has been around for as
long as recorded civilization, but other things, including emotional
horror of the subject, have kept it largely under wraps.

Pederasts seem to be eternal adolescents in their erotic life. They
become fixated upon the youth and sexual vitality of the adolescent
boy. The budding sexuality of the boy can be fascinating to watch.
Many pederasts speak with wistfulness of the boy's sexual vigor, his
unbridled enthusiasm in sexual experimentation, and his ecstacy and
sheer joy in sexual fulfillment. Pederasts love the boy in themselves
and themselves in the boy. It may be a way to preserve youth and
sexual vitality.

Types of Pederasts

Not all pederasts are the same, and many subtypes can be distinguished.
All the variations are not known, but some have been crudely de-
lineated by Rossman as follows.[2]

The first type is substitute pederasty. This involves mutual sex play
among normal males temporarily separated from females, for example,
sailors, tourists, prisoners, and so forth. Rossman suggests that over 2
million American men may fall into this category. It involves a simulated effort to meet erotic and emotional needs by pretending the boy
sex-object is actually a woman.

Sexual contacts in prisons often involve youthful inmates who are
raped. (In Philadelphia, teen-age boys were raped in the sheriff's van
transporting prisoners to courtrooms for their hearings.) It is doubtful
that these prison sexual contacts are sexually motivated. There is a
strong element of the homosexual sex act being used to humiliate,
dominate, and intimidate young prisoners. It is a display of sadistic
power rather than a sexual act. As elsewhere in our culture, sex is used
as an aggressive weapon.

A second type of pederast is the tutor in sex, in which older males
teach sex to adolescent boys. These types often work with adolescents
(teachers, youth workers, social club leaders, and so forth) and are
usually not far out of adolescence themselves. The emphasis is on
giving pleasure to the boy, perhaps to the exclusion of the tutor's own
sexual satisfaction.

It is often this tutor relationship that others see as seducing a boy into homosexuality. However, Rossman suggests that the relationship may have quite the opposite effect. His hypothesis is that a pederast relationship with a masculine man directs boys away from confirming a homosexual identity and into normal heterosexuality! It should be stressed that the cases in which this may be so are those in which the boy is not forced to play a feminized role.

Paul Goodman relates his experience when a boy came to his bed one night. Goodman sent the boy away. The disappointed boy informed the school authorities of Goodman's involvement with other boys, and he was fired from his teaching job. Goodman commented: "Had I taken him to bed for a few minutes of affectionate sex, he might have been a better and more compassionate boy. He was jealous because everyone knew I had a favorite. I taught him to dance, how to court a girl, and when he was embarrassed at his fumbling attempts at lovemaking and came to me with his embarrassment, I sent him back with confidence and contraceptives."[3]

Rossman cites a number of examples of delinquent boys, especially those involved in sadistic, aggressive behavior, who were turned around in their behavior by the sexual love of a compassionate man. One poignant example involved a court social worker who rescued a number of boys by taking them to bed with him. A grateful community honored him for his work with the delinquent boys. He was in a quandary, however, as to how to tell people that his miracles were brought about through sex. This sensitive and tortured man finally resolved his dilemma by committing suicide.

While professionals certainly wouldn't recommend sexual therapy for delinquents, in some cases it probably does work. It might succeed for boys neglected and deprived of the affection of a father in their homes. These children crave masculine attention, and some have learned that sex is one way to get close to another person, to be held, to be loved, and to be warm. When the sex is pleasurable, as it usually is, the child is reinforced by the fulfillment of his more infantile needs.

Any child who is neglected and starved for affection becomes a high risk for sexual exploitation by adults. The runaway boy on the street and the foster child are two examples. It is easy for these children, deprived of the love of a father, to turn to sex with men to get the fathering they never had. While the tutor in sex may believe he has the child's best interests at heart, other men, not as scrupulous, may exploit the child for their own sexual satisfaction.

Some professionals view men who engage in sex with young boys as also motivated by a need for fathering. They may act out the role of the giving father they wished they'd had as a child, while at the same time identifying with the boys. They do unto others as they wish had been done unto them—to be loved by a father. Through sex with boys, they try to capture vicariously a joy that eluded them as children.

A third type of pederast is the sports comrade, the super-masculine, athletic man who trains boys to be tough and masculine. Individuals of this type may become sports coaches, perhaps in schools or various community organized sports programs for boys. The desire for intercourse with the boys is sublimated into roughhouse and mutual masturbation. Into this category might fall the fathers in Los Angeles who reputedly slept with one another's sons on camping trips.

Another type of pederast is the adventurer, a person who seeks varied sexual experiences. He may become involved with boys with the attitude of "I'll try anything once."

Another type is the sensuous pederast who uses the boy for his own sexual pleasures. This type has a long history in our culture, the "pastime of sultans and kings." This pederast seeks an erotic experience different from that obtained with women. His motto might be, "A woman for love and children, but a boy for pleasure."

Another type is the viciously exploitative pederast. Constituting less than 1 percent of all pederasts, these men seduce boys through drugs, alcohol, and pornography. They may kidnap, abuse, and then prostitute their victims. This group thrives during police crackdowns on boy prostitution because the scarcity of boys drives the price up, making the risks well worth it to the pederast.

Another group is the fantasy and fetish pederasts. These are probably also few in number. They substitute other experiences for the anal intercourse they desire with boys. There is, for example, an underwear cult that buys underwear worn by young boys and uses it as part of their masturbation ritual. Others like to watch boys being given enemas, spanked, or held in bondage. There are specialized porno magazines and books catering to these narrow tastes.

The above types of pederasts are only roughly described. They tell us nothing about dynamics or etiology. Few pederasts fit neatly into one type. Most are combinations of types, and even that may change in a particular individual over the course of his life.

Is Pederasty Abuse?

There are some pederasts who openly advocate that man-boy love should be made legal. Through newsletters and magazines that circulate through a loose network around the country, they share their views with other like-minded men. Drawing on a long history of man-boy love, they justify their attitude toward teen-age boys as one of adoration. They see themselves as indulging the boy's needs for masculine companionship and gratifying their sexual needs. They stress their high-minded devotion to the welfare of the boys they love.

Some men will adopt a boy, perhaps pay for his education, help him get a job, and encourage him to become a useful citizen. All, of course, in return for sex. A group of bankers in the Midwest selected a junior-high-school boy every other year for a full-expense college scholarship. It was understood that he would take turns sleeping with them over the next two years.

Some pederasts would claim that their relationships with boys are not exploitative or abusive. In the above case, for example, the boys received college scholarships. "Was not what they received of far more value than what they gave," these men would argue.

It is not uncommon in some foreign cultures for a family to give or loan their son to a rich American for sexual purposes with the hope that the wealthy patron will want to educate the boy.

Though most parents in America would not trade their son's sexual favors for a benefit to the boy or to themselves, the House hearings on sexual exploitation of children contain a number of examples of parents who did sell their sons for sexual purposes in exchange for money, property, or other items of value. Some parents accepted money in return for letting their children be photographed in pornographic movies. But what if the child is over fourteen and agrees that this is something he wants to do in return for money, a trip to Mexico, or a college education? Is this exploitation?

There are no easy answers to these questions. One issue involved here is the age of consent for sexual activities, particularly the right of adolescents to control their own sexual lives.

There are those who would say no child under eighteen can consent to any sexual relationship. Others would set the age at sixteen, or fourteen, or even twelve. Some child libertarians would take the extreme view that a child of any age has the right to his own sexual life and to engage in whatever sexual activity an adult can legally engage in.[4] The point is, there is a diversity of opinion on this issue. Our society needs to reconsider and reevaluate its sexual standards for children of all ages, particularly for its teen-agers. This group more than any other needs some kind of legal sexual outlet.

A second issue is the one of harm to the child. There are those that believe that any form of sexual contact for a child is abusive and harmful, especially same sex contacts. There is no supporting evidence that this is universally true.

Many of the children discussed in this section and elsewhere in this book did not consider their sexual contacts with adults to be abusive. Many of the males in this chapter would not consider themselves abused. One of the problems in police prosecution of adult offenders is that often the police are unable to get the boys to testify against the men involved. This is true especially if the boy was treated with respect, kindness, or tenderness by the adult. To a poor boy from a deprived background, perhaps without a father, $100 a night, a trip to Mexico, or a motorbike looks pretty good. How can such a child be convinced that he has been abused or exploited?

Any harm in sexual contacts depends upon the child's age, vulnerability, previous experiences, general adjustment, lack of violence or force in the sexual contact, what the child received besides sex, and how the child deals with the experience. Contrary to popular opinion, a sexual experience is not upsetting to many children. Unfortunately, there is no way of knowing beforehand what the effect of a sexual experience will be on the child. After the fact, it is easy to say that the experience was traumatic, that the child is showing symptoms of distress, and hence it can be inferred that the experience was upsetting. It is also difficult to trace symptoms to the sexual incident per se. Some of the supposed effects seen may be due to other factors in the child's life situation: abuse, neglect, exposure to family violence, inadequate parenting, and so forth. The likelihood of trauma to the child increases greatly when the child is pressured into sex against his will, where there is injury or pain, where the offender involved is a close relative, or where there is clear exploitation (for example, by a pimp).

Take the case of the Midwest bankers cited earlier and compare it with the following. A fourteen-year-old runaway arrives at the bus station of a large city. He is met by a man who offers him a room for the night. The boy accepts and goes with the man. He is raped, drugged, and turned out on the streets as a prostitute. He brings in $300 a night, 60 percent of which is kept by his pimp, the man who met him at the bus station. The boy contracts VD twice during his two years as a prostitute.

Both cases involve illegal sex acts with boys. They differ on the issues of consent, victimization, force, exploitation, harm, and potential trauma. These issues need to be addressed by society. To focus simply on the illegal sex is to obscure much. Untouched is the deprivation that makes a college scholarship such a strong inducement to a boy, or the family emotional deprivation that drives a boy to run away. Even more deeply buried is the secret need that drives some men to seek out young boys for sex.

Chapter XI
Molestation

In the very few studies that report offenses involving male children, at least half or more of the victims are under ten years of age—the largest group being those between six and nine years old.[1] The dynamics of child molesters who select young males under nine or ten years of age are probably different from those who select teen-aged boys. But, on the whole, these child molesters may be classified into two groups—the nonviolent and the violent child molester.

The Nonviolent Child Molester

Molesters of young children are probably psychologically children themselves. They identify more easily with children and feel more comfortable in their presence. They often view adults in a very negative fashion. The child molester may feel like a child himself when in the presence of adults, and perhaps more like an adult when involved with a child. Children are nonthreatening sexual objects to the child molester, and he usually does not threaten or harm them. It is possible that a certain amount of gender confusion is involved in those cases where persons are attracted to male children.

Sexual molestation of young males may be an attempt by the adult molester to deal with a traumatic sexual event in his own childhood. As a result of the childhood trauma, the molester's psychosexual development is arrested at the prepubertal level. He is, in effect, psychosexually immature. One of the immaturities that is often noted is that child molesters are found to have had much less sexual experience than normal people. In the case of those molesters who prefer their own sex, there probably has been less than the normal amount of opposite-sex play experiences in their childhood years.

The large majority of child molesters are gentle with their victims. Their interaction with their victims is immature and playful, as if between two children. They do not generally represent a threat to the well-being of their victims. In the case of brief, single contacts, there probably is no great trauma to the victim and little in the way of lasting, harmful aftereffects. The hysterical reactions of parents to a male child who has been molested is far out of proportion to the seriousness of the experience, and probably is more responsible for causing psychological upset to the child than was the sexual experience itself. The typical molester of male children rarely progresses to more violent attacks on his victims. A lack of force is more his style, and he relies on inducements and seduction to attract the child.

In their book *The Personality of a Child Molester,* A. P. Bell and C. S. Hall recount the childhood trauma of incest that took place in the life of their subject. At the age of four, the subject was forced by his father to suck his penis. In the subject's own words:

I felt bewildered. The size of his erection frightened me. I had never been approached like that before by my father. . . . All I can remember is my father's hypnotic, angry stare as I tried to push his penis away from my face.[2]

Although traumatized by the initial experience, the boy came to enjoy the unusual attention he received from his father. The activity went on for some time until the father left the family. A major result of these incestual acts was an identity crisis from which the boy never recovered.

In later life, when the subject began molesting young children of both sexes, he did not involve them in oral-genital sex. He was careful, gentle, and considerate with the children. His behavior was often covert so that the children were hardly aware of the sexual pleasure he obtained. It would seem that he attempted to make his activities every bit as untraumatic to the children as his had been traumatic to him. It is as if he said, "This is how it should have been, not frightening as it was for me."

In the case of Bell and Hall's patient, the childhood sexual trauma was probably more than offset by the positive attention and enjoyment he received. As a result, when he became an adult who molested children, his behavior did not contain a strong element of hostility toward his victims, but was more an undoing of an early trauma and a replaying of the pleasurable aspects of his childhood experience.

The presence of pleasure and a relative lack of trauma may have much to do with shaping an adult's nonviolent interest in young boys. In April 1978, poet Allen Ginsberg stated, in a live interview on WCVB-TV in Boston, that he had a sexual preference for "young boys." Ginsberg went on to discuss how, at the age of eight, he was sexually molested by an older man in his grandfather's candy store in Revere. According to a report in the Boston *Globe,* the poet stated that he had found the experience enjoyable.

Of course, an early childhood sexual experience with a male is probably not the sole determinant in developing an adult interest in young boys. However, it is very possible that if the experience is benign, the later adult behavior toward young boys will be nonviolent.

The Violent Child Molester

What if the childhood sexual trauma consists of force and violence? The child who is the victim of a sadistic sexual assault may indeed show lasting psychological harm. The child may come to identify with his childhood aggressor. *If,* in his subsequent sexual development, he becomes an adult with an interest in young boys, the chances are very good that he will be a violent child molester. He will then do unto other children as was done unto him.

The following are some typical examples of this type of sexual attack:

In Boston, a twelve-year-old boy was abducted and sexually assaulted while delivering newspapers early in the morning. Taken forcibly to an isolated section of a park, the boy was made to undress and then raped. He was forced to commit an unnatural act [fellatio], then beaten and stabbed with an ice pick. The offender, who was not caught, was thought to be a seventeen-or-eighteen-year-old male.[3]

A thirty-four-year-old former fifth-grade teacher and Boy Scout leader was convicted of kidnapping, assaulting with a pistol, and sexually abusing a fifteen-year-old boy. Though he pleaded innocent to this charge, the man pleaded guilty to other charges of sexually assaulting four boys, all under fourteen years of age.[4]

Of course the history of these men is not known, so one can only hypothesize that they experienced a violent sexual assault in their childhood. It is likely, however, that the violence was the greater trauma. One man, raped by his father and five brothers, sodomized young boys when he became an adult. His repetitive behavior was a perverted attempt to understand how people who love you can hurt you by committing a painful act.

A twenty-nine-year-old man was sent to prison for sodomizing four teen-aged boys. He came to understand that his feelings of inadequacy led to his abusive sexual behavior. "I was put down [as a child] ... so I put them down," he said. Sex was not even important to him. Instead, the helplessness of a child was converted to an adult's power to put down others. When he humiliated young boys by forcing them into anal sex, he became powerful—no longer the humiliated child. He revenged himself upon the abusers in his past by abusing others.

Molesters, Homosexuals, and the Schools

In spite of the fact that a child molester selects a male victim, he usually does not consider himself to be homosexual. It is not unusual for a child molester to express strong feelings against homosexuals. One child molester, interviewed in prison, stated that he sometimes had sex with women, but men turned him off. He let the interviewer know very definitely that consenting sex between adult males was not normal. This offender had raped two boys, age ten and twelve, forcing them into fellatio and sodomy.[5] Raping two boys was normal, but sex between consenting men was unnatural!

As the example shows, not even child molesters are immune to homophobia. That being the case, one cannot expect the public to be less immune. A recent concern of the public has been to protect school children from those teachers who are suspected of being sexually interested in males. This is translated into keeping the homosexuals out of the schools, as witnessed by the recent campaign in California organized by a politician and purveyor of orange juice. Contrary to popular belief, there is little reason why a homosexual should be a sexual threat to young boys. The argument is used that a homosexual is not a proper masculine role model. It is unlikely that mere contact with a homosexual by a male over six years of age is going to change an already established sexual preference.

What has been overlooked in this preoccupation with the homosexual teacher is that male teachers attacked female students more

frequently than they attacked male students. Any group seriously interested in the sexual safety of children in the classroom would do well
to concentrate on pedophiles—men sexually interested in young children, regardless of the sex.

Molesters and Youth Organizations

Any man who has a sexual interest in young boys will gravitate to those
places where young boys congregate. This includes public and private
schools, youth organizations, residential homes for children, community sports programs, public beaches, youth detention homes and
prisons, plus the traditional playgrounds, candy stores, and pool halls.

Offenders have often been associated with a youth organization
such as the Boy Scouts, YMCA, Big Brothers, or Boys' Clubs. This is
not to imply that these organizations or the men who work for them do
not provide a generous service to boys. But, by their very nature, these
organizations attract some men who are sexually interested in young
males. Note the following examples of Boy Scout leaders found guilty
of sexual offenses:

In Massachusetts, two Boy Scout leaders were arrested on sixty-
one morals charges against three twelve-year-old boys. One was a thirty-
six-year-old district director and the other a twenty-three-year-old
assistant Scoutmaster. The two men lived together. Both men posted
bonds, jumped bail, and fled the state to avoid prosecution.[6]

A fifty-two-year-old decorated Boy Scout leader was sentenced
to fifteen to twenty-five years in prison for three charges, one of statutory rape, involving eight- and nine-year-old Cub Scouts. This offender
had been paroled from state prison seven years earlier after serving
nearly seventeen years for sexual offenses against children.[7]

Even if all such men could be screened out, young males would
still not be safe. Surprising as it may seem, otherwise normal adult
males who work with young boys can often, quite inexplicably, find
themselves becoming sexually aroused. These men, to their own surprise and horror, become sexually involved with a boy, sometimes with
devastating results to their psyches. Whether or not one believes that
every man has suppressed desires toward young males, the exuberant
sexuality of a pubescent boy can be a threat to a normal adult male.
The boy's capacity for pleasure can stimulate the man's own suppressed
sexuality. Adolescents are especially prone to sexual problems—it is

after all the major developmental issue with which they grapple—and the sympathy of a concerned and affectionate man may well result in sexual arousal in either the boy, the man, or both.

Few social service and charitable agencies are willing to face the fact that quite normal men can be aroused sexually by young boys. That they are is not evidence of homosexuality, but may even be evidence of their humaneness and sensitivity. Such a reaction does not mean that the man is not fit to work with boys. A man who is not conscious of these temptations is a much poorer risk than a man who is aware of such temptations and openly tries to deal with them.

Rossman cites the policy statement of an unnamed youth services agency which adopted the most sensible approach to the problem that I have seen.[8] The statement quite directly says that many men are not aware of their own capacity to be sexually aroused by young boys. While recognizing such arousal is not necessarily an indication of homosexuality, the agency will not tolerate any sexual contact between staff and children.

The statement goes on to offer counseling to any staff member, at no cost, to help him deal with such a problem. In the case of an actual discovered sexual contact, the policy for a first offense is to offer either a chance to resign or to enter into a program of counseling and therapy. The statement further encourages friendly and natural physical contact between men and boys and stresses it should not be avoided because one is uptight about homosexuality. The agency also requires inservice training for staff on homosexuality and counseling in which efforts are made to help the staff interpret to the children the sexual feelings of both staff and children. Concerned adult males who can answer children's questions about sexual matters without embarrassment, and who can deal comfortably with the sex play that goes on naturally between adolescents are seen by the agency as positive contributors to the mental health of the children.

It is unfortunate that there are not more agencies and individuals who can take this straightforward and sensible attitude toward sexuality and sexual contacts between staff and children.

Chapter XII
Male Sex Rings

Most pederasts and child molesters prefer anonymity and secretiveness. Sometimes they cautiously seek out other men who share their interests in young boys. This association of like-minded men may grow and become a loosely organized group in a geographical area. Sometimes the chain of associations spreads out, perhaps even stretching across the country.

Every now and then, one of these groups of men is uncovered by the police. The state prosecutor and newspapers may speak of a sex ring, implying a degree of organization beyond the association of like-minded people. Sometimes the "ring" is an invention of the police and press and is nowhere nearly as well organized as implied. Other times, the description of a ring is well-founded, with the procurement of boys, the delivery of services, and the network of customers all highly organized.

The phenomenon of the male sex ring is unique. One seldom sees such an organized group involving female sex victims. In the last century, in New York City and other large metropolitan areas, one could find specialized houses of prostitution catering to those with a taste for young female children (young boys were also available). Before the passage of the Mann Act, the organized sex ring of young females would involve considerable trafficking in females across state lines. Today, such an organization of females is rare. The same is not true, however, for males.

Every now and then a story will make the newspapers about a sex ring consisting of middle-aged men who have been having sex with boys. Some of the cities in which such rings have been recently exposed are Boise, Idaho; Los Angeles and Santa Clara, California; Waukesha, Wisconsin; Houston, Texas; and Boston, Massachusetts.

The fascinating Boise incident was the topic of S. Gerassi's book, *The Boys of Boise*. As a sociological study of homophobia in a small town, the book is very well done. Over 500 suspects were turned up, and eleven men went to prison for from six months to life. A wealthy professional man, reputed to be the "Queen" of the ring, never was publicly exposed. The town went from cracking down on sex with young boys to persecuting homosexual activities between consenting adults (presumably on the assumption that all homosexuals are interested in boys).

In November 1973, a ring in Los Angeles involved fourteen adults charged with ninety crimes against boys under thirteen years of age (the youngest was six). Involved in this case was the production of pornographic books and magazines as well as movies.[1]

In Santa Clara, police broke up a local ring involving a highschool teacher and a free-lance photographer who ran a porno picture ring. Over 250 boys were said to be involved stretching over a ten-year period. Police confiscated over 10,000 pornographic pictures, though the photographer had already destroyed over four times that number.[2]

The incidents in Waukesha occurred in 1960 and again in 1974. It is interesting that in these and other such rings, the men involved are often middle- and upper-class professionals. The offenders were physicians, a pediatrician, teachers, a surgeon, and businessmen. There were stories of wild parties and orgies held in an isolated farmhouse.

In San Francisco, police uncovered a child prostitution ring involving thirty boys. The children were taken to customers in different parts of the city and exhibited naked—"like livestock," according to one police officer. The man who was charged with running the ring was a convicted child molester.[3]

The Boston Homosexual Ring

In December 1977, a large-scale sex ring involving young boys was reportedly broken up by the Suffolk County district attorney's office in Boston. The investigation made the afternoon news that I heard on the car radio on my way home. The evening newspaper carried considerably more detail.[4] One of the men indicted was an investment counselor who lived on the same street as I did.

Twenty-four men, including a psychiatrist, a psychologist, a num-ber of educators, and a former Washington lobbyist, were indicted. The Revere-based ring used as many as sixty-three young boys, aged eight to thirteen, for homosexual acts and as models for pornographic photos and movies. (Apparently the visual dimension is important in many such male sex rings, with photos and movies being made of the sexual acts. Rossman reports 75 percent of all pederasts collect photos.)[5]

The boys supposedly were given marijuana and beer, shown movies of sexual activity between men and women, and then coaxed into sexual relationships with the men. The men paid between $30 and $50 per visit with the boys, and the children received between $5 and $10 for taking part. The male clients came to Revere from all over the East Coast, according to the newspaper account. Several of the boys involved were reported to be state wards.

The case came to light during an investigation following an arrest the previous spring of a Boston school bus driver indicted for twenty-seven counts of rape, including assault with intent to rape a female child. This man had a long record of sexual assaults on children. He was finally sentenced to state prison for life for attempts to rape a ten- and a thirteen-year-old girl, and for other acts involving five boys between the ages of twelve and fifteen. He is currently serving twenty-three life sentences for rape.

Investigation of the case led to the arrest of a Revere man whose apartment was allegedly used for the activities of the ring. This man had paid the bus driver to bring children to his apartment. He was ul-timately convicted and sentenced to three fifteen-to-twenty-five-year prison terms for the rape of three youngsters.

When the man's apartment was raided, police found more than 100 photographs of naked boys, pornographic movie films, and several address books. Through this material and with the cooperation of some of the boys identified from the pictures, police were able to iden-tify many of the men involved.

According to the boys, their sexual contacts in the man's apart-ment had been going on for one or two years, sometimes with the same men. Officials said most of the boys were from broken homes with no male image. It was rumored that one boy had been transported to the West Coast to take part in making a pornographic movie. The DA's office promised more arrests in the future.

A few days later police announced that another man, a former volunteer worker with a Boy Scout troop in nearby Charlestown, had been arrested in connection with the case. (This incident is reported on page 93 of this book; it later turned out that this man had no connection whatsoever with the Boston ring.) A week later, two more men were arraigned. One was a Connecticut florist, and the other the former bus driver whose arrest sparked the entire probe. He was brought from jail to the court for arraignment on one charge of rape, and immediately returned to jail. There was a short item in the paper that a Boston minister would be arrested imminently, but there never was a follow-up story to indicate that he had been.

For all basic purposes, that ended the media coverage of the ring. There had been two days of major stories and a few scattered short items in the next few months. No new arrests were reported, and the case dropped out of the public eye. In a letter to the editor in the Boston *Globe,* 20 December 1977, a member of Boston's gay community deplored the actions of the members of the sex ring. "The gay community," he said, "does not condone the actions of the real perverts." The writer continued, "It is one thing to be gay, but totally another to be sick like these men." He hoped the public would not link the gay community with this "travesty."[6]

On March 1, one of the indicted persons—a former Boston city employee—was sentenced to two eight-to-twelve-year terms in state prison for the rape of two young boys (rape in this case was performing oral sex on the two boys). In court, the man's history of "heterosexual orientation" and his experience as a coach of Little League softball and hockey were read to the court.

On May 1, the Boston child psychiatrist indicted in the case requested a delay in his trial because of extensive publicity that another aspect of the case had received. His request was denied. The remainder of the men have yet to come to trial.

There was every indication from the newspaper and from other sources that the Revere ring was very well organized and greater in scope than the twenty-four men who were indicted. Yet, for all practical purposes, the investigation produced no more indictments. One cannot help but wonder why the case died a very premature death.

R. Lloyd, in his book *For Money or Love,* says that sex rings usually are not reported by the press. The police will often run the culprits out of town and not prosecute, especially if an important adult is involved; this may be more true in small towns. There were rumors in the Boston case that some of the boys in the case had disappeared and could not be found. Sadism and murder do occur now and then in sex rings, but there is no concrete evidence, as far as the public knows, that such was the case in the Boston ring.

Mark Rowland in his article "The Revere Case: Not What It Was Cracked Up to Be," suggested that the Boston/Revere ring was more fiction than fact, existing mainly in the minds of the police. The media simply reported what the DA's office told them without any attempt to evaluate the story independently. The basic facts were there, but their interpretation was a distortion of reality. If I had to sum up Rowland's view in a single quote, it would be this one. "It has become increasingly clear that most of the claims bandied about by the DA's office (District Attorney Garrett Byrne) were outright distortions, exploiting the considerable reserve of homophobia that has always existed in Irish-Catholic Boston."[7]

Consider how the case looks in light of Rowland's findings:

1. Of the twenty-four men indicted, only seventeen had some connection with the Revere group. The other seven indicted for acts against male children were individual cases *not* connected with the others. They were lumped together with the implication that they were all part of one ring. This tended to inflate the importance of the "ring," a phenomenon that is often a police or newspaper invention.

2. The seventeen men indicted (plus the three with whom the case began a few years ago), brought the number arrested to twenty. The other four men indicted have never been identified. Rowland suggests that these names are simply fabrications.

3. There is no indication in any of the reports that the case involved either forced sex or molestation. While the men were supposed to be charged with rape, many were charged with lesser offenses (unnatural acts, indecent assault), or not at all. The statutory rape charge is a technical one, involving a minor under sixteen years of age. It does not imply force, violence, or lack of consent. (Legally the "victims" cannot consent).

4. The DA's office implied that these indictments were but the tip of an iceberg, and that many more indictments were to follow. The fact is that since the original indictments in December 1977, no *new* indictments have been made. In spite of the DA's hopes for speedy trials, and the promise to give these cases special priority, only two of the men have yet come to trial. According to Rowland, the prosecution is quietly letting defense lawyers know that they will not,

in many instances, object to motions for lengthy delays of the trials.

Three men did receive jail terms, but two were tried and sentenced in October 1977, before the case broke in December, and the third was already awaiting trial in November. He was finally tried and sentenced in March 1978.

In December 1978, almost a year after the Boston/Revere case broke in the news, the first of the new defendants was brought to trial. The man, a fifty-year-old psychiatrist, was accused of statutory rape of a fifteen-year-old boy. The doctor's defense was that he was conducting research on male prostitution. After a two-week trial, he was convicted of four counts of statutory rape and sentenced to five years probation, on the condition he undergo psychiatric treatment. The prosecutor had asked for a sentence of five to seven years in a state prison. The maximum penalty for conviction could have been life.

5. The implication at the time was that a nationwide network of child porn had been broken. This was later modified to an East Coast network! In fact, all but five of the men were from Massachusetts. One, arrested in Florida, was later conceded by the DA's office not to have been a part of the Revere ring. Another from Georgia had formerly lived in Revere. The East Coast "network," then, consisted of a man from New York City, one from Bridgeport, Connecticut, and one from Baltimore.

6. No connection with pornography has been established. There were ten films and over 100 pictures confiscated from the house in Revere, and while of a sexual nature, there was no evidence that they were for commercial sale rather than personal use. As mentioned elsewhere in this book, it is common practice for male pedophiles to collect photos of the boys with whom they are involved.

7. The day the news broke, the DA's office set up a hot line for citizens to call in any information about the Revere case or any other incident of sex between men and boys. Over 100 phone calls were received, most of them anonymous. The Massachusetts Civil Liberties Union brought a class action suit to halt the use of the hot line, and the DA's office dropped the practice.[8] The hot line was a gross violation of civil rights and an invitation to a witch-hunt.

8. According to Rowland, the majority of the boys involved were state wards. (This is something I suspected but was unable to confirm.) The complaints against the men did not originate with the boys. Instead the boys were sought out by the police and encouraged to turn state's witnesses (Rowland says they were "accosted" and "intimidated").

That is where the situation now stands. The DA's office has lost much of its credibility. According to Rowland, if the age of consent for sex were set at fourteen, nearly all the Revere cases would be elimi-nated.

The Revere case sounds more like "boy-love" or hustling than child molestation. According to Rowland, "Whatever money had been ex-changed between men and boys had been irregular and largely inci-dental to the sex." The DA's handling of the case has, in my opinion, obscured three issues that need to be faced:

> The offender-victim approach obscures the fact that hustling is a consenting relationship, and as much economic and psychological as sexual. Should the law be involved in consenting relationships in which there is no force, violence, or exploitation for profit if the child is over fourteen years of age?

> Boy-love is a fact of life, and instead of treating those involved as criminals, the question of when a teen-ager has a right to determine his own sexual life needs to be faced. Existing laws are contradictory and archaic. Denying children any bonds of affection may be more damaging to their psychological development than involvement in a boy-love situation.

> A third issue, perhaps relative to these cases, is that gay teen-agers who are state wards cannot be placed in gay foster homes under the present policy of the Department of Public Welfare.[9] Perhaps the concern is over possible sexual exploitation. Whether or not this is a realistic concern needs to be studied and examined.

It would be better for society to face these issues and make rational decisions than to obscure them with public hysteria.

Fallout from the Boston/Revere Case   The day after the case broke in the newspapers, I spoke with the parents of a ten-year-old boy whom I see in therapy. They asked if I had read the papers and heard about the case. When I said I had, they asked what I thought of it. I made a neutral comment to the effect that I thought it was something that happened to a lot of boys. They then proceeded to tell me how their son had been raped at five years of age by a teen-ager in the neighbor-hood. They wondered if this trauma could have been responsible for any of the boy's current difficulties (it probably was not).

A week after the case first came to public attention, the Suffolk County DA announced that he would seek tougher rules for picking foster parents. His logic is a bit difficult to follow. Apparently, a num-ber of the boys were state wards. It is not clear just how many were, and no official number has been released. I heard that a computer search was being made of the names of the boys involved to try to determine just how many of the boys were foster children, but I doubt that the public will ever find out the results.

While some of the children may have been foster children, none of the defendants were identified publicly as foster parents. One victim had been placed by a state agency (but not the Welfare Department) in the home of one of the men supposedly involved in the Boston ring. The DA, nonetheless, said he would seek to amend the law which prohibits state agencies from investigating whether or not individuals who apply to become foster parents have convictions for child abuse crimes or other crimes detrimental to the moral fiber of young children. (To my knowledge, a year later, this still has not been done.)

A week after the Boston ring was uncovered the Boston *Globe* reported that a statewide telephone hot line for child abuse cases was being recommended by the Massachusetts House Subcommittee on Children in Need of Services. The need for a hot line was tied directly to the recent investigation of the sex ring scandal. Hearings were subsequently held on the matter of a hot line. Representatives from the Department of Public Welfare spoke against the hot line. Their argument was that if the hot line were installed, the department would be unable to handle the increase in cases that would result! Rather than request more money and extra workers, the state would prefer not to know about child abuse cases.

Two days after the press coverage of the case, it was reported that the detective who directed the investigation into the sex ring would meet with the Department of Public Welfare to determine how society could help the young victims. The detective's approach was most enlightened. "We've got to figure out who's going to handle the fall-out from this case," he said. "Who's going to help these kids? This is a social problem and we want to figure out what public services are needed by these kids." His attitude stood in contrast to that of the Commissioner of Welfare, as reported in a telephone interview with the Boston *Globe*. According to the commissioner, no department-run foster home was involved, none of the defendants were foster parents, and he expected that the number of boys who were wards of the state would be a very small proportion of the total number of boys involved.[10]

The public has never been told whether the commissioner's expectations were confirmed or not. I have heard from other sources that in fact the number of foster children was substantial. There was also no further information in the paper about any state help for the victims or of any activities on the part of the DPW on the victims' behalf.

One final note on the fall-out from the case: the chief justice of the Massachusetts superior court had been in trouble for some time over a number of alleged irregularities in his behavior. He was the man who would be selecting the judges to preside at the trials of the men arrested in the Boston sex ring. In April 1978, the judge attended a lecture in Boston by Gore Vidal. The lecture was sponsored by the Boston/Boise Committee, a gay rights organization, as a fund-raiser for the twenty-four defendants in the Boston sex ring case.[11] In spite of the judge's claim that he had no idea of the fund-raising nature of the event, the hue and cry raised in the media resulted in the suspension of the judge from his post. His conduct in a number of areas was investigated by the superior court. He was ultimately censured by the court, and the governor requested his resignation. The judge refused, and a special session of the Legislature was convened to remove the judge. Both houses voted to do so. Early in August 1978, the judge quit his post.

When one looks back on the Boston sex ring scandal, one can't help but ask, "What has changed?" A few men have been sent to jail, and presumably a few others may suffer the same fate. Their lives will be in danger there, for the child molester is treated by other prisoners as scum. It is not uncommon for them to be forcibly raped by the other inmates, who no doubt feel very virtuous about doing so. The men will probably not get much in the way of psychiatric help, but then neither will most of the victims. Sometime in the future, Boston will uncover a new boys-for-sale sex ring. Everyone will be properly shocked and ask, "How can such a thing happen?" Two months later, it, too, will all be forgotten unless measures are taken to understand the full nature of the problem.

Violence in Sex Rings

The sex ring in Houston was famous for its violence. It set a record (since broken) for the greatest number of victims in a mass murder. Over 300 boys were involved, and at least twenty-seven of them are known

to have been tortured and killed. This ring differed from others of its
kind in that it mainly involved one man and his two accomplices. The
story of the Houston murders is detailed in J. Olsen's book *The Man
with the Candy.*

The Houston case raises one particular area of concern. One often
hears the comment that homosexuals, or at least men who have sex
with boys, are prone to violence. The gruesome Houston murders are
cited as evidence. The boys were tortured on a special board, sodomized,
and sexually mutilated. One corpse was recovered with the boy's penis
and testicles wrapped in a small plastic bag beside the body. Another
victim's penis was gnawed nearly in two.

This type of lust murder makes spectacular reading, but whether
the victims are male or female, offenses of this sort are fortunately rare.
The sadistic sex assault involves the dangerous combination of sex and
aggression. Aggression is eroticized, and the sexual abuse of the victim
involves cruelty and anger. Torture is often involved, as if the victim
were being punished. The victim may be a stand-in for the offender
who is punishing some part of himself that he hates.

Contrary to the usual belief, the lust-type offense is not an impulsive act but rather a premeditated one. Much planning goes into selecting the victim and fantasizing what will be done to him or her.
Sexual release is secondary to the intent to hurt, degrade, and ultimately to destroy the "bad" child. The aggression stimulates the offender sexually, and this in turn provokes more aggression. The two
emotions escalate until they culminate in the death of the victim. This
type of offender is an extremely dangerous one, and rehabilitation is
very difficult.

As to whether homosexual violence is any more common than
heterosexual violence, the answer is probably "no." It may even be less
common. The use of force or violence by homosexuals in their sexual
relationships is rare, except for that small group of sadomasochists.
Rarely do contacts by homosexuals with children, when they do occur,
utilize force or violence. D. J. West, in his study of homosexuality,
concluded that there is no firm evidence that a homosexual orientation
has any connection with homicidal sadism.[12]

Some people claim that sadism and violence are common features
of male sex rings, but in the examples I have found, this has not been
true. One example that alluded to sadism was the following report from
the *New York Times.*[13] In November 1973, in Jersey City, three men

and a woman were arrested on morals charges involving alleged homosexual activities with teen-age boys. The defendants were supposedly connected with a New York group of nautical cadets. The organization provided recreational activities for boys between the ages of five and eighteen. The boys were dressed in uniforms and taken for boat rides. One of the defendants had apparently been authorized to establish a Jersey City branch of the organization.

The prosecutor's office said that pornographic literature and pictures were confiscated during the arrest, along with devices "related to homosexual activities." No mention was made as to what those devices were, but in a subsequent one sentence paragraph, it was stated that "whips and brass knuckles" were confiscated.

Whips and brass knuckles are no more standard equipment for homosexual activities than they are for heterosexual activities. This is sadomasochism—which occurs among both heterosexuals and homosexuals—and, where pursued with serious intent, is one of the most serious kinds of abuse against children.

Other Types of Sex Rings

In Hauppauge, Long Island, eight men, including a child psychiatrist and a former organizer for Big Brothers of New York, were indicted for their part in a homosexual ring described as "international" in scope.[14] The last is probably an exaggeration and is based on the fact that the psychiatrist was from Northern Ireland, that one of the boys was brought from Puerto Rico, and that one of those indicted was a fugitive from Ontario currently sought by Interpol throughout Central Europe.

Involved in the sex "club" were fifteen boys, from ten to fifteen years of age. Some were described as "fatherless boys from deprived areas" who were paid in "candy and pens" for their sexual behavior. No attempt was made to restrain the boys or keep them from going home.

The men were indicted on twenty-seven counts of conspiracy, sodomy, and sexual abuse, following a two-year investigation. Big Brothers of New York admitted that the man who had organized for them was "in charge of group recreational activities," but denied that he had "direct contact with any children during his employment." Police were investigating the possibility of fraudulent use of the group's name to attract children.

Almost all of the men involved in this case were married. One was the father of three teen-age children. The major sexual orientation of these men was heterosexual, but privately they preferred young boys.

While the men obviously exploited the children's need to be loved, perhaps they, too, were looking for a kind of fathering. Their inability to separate love, caring, and emotional closeness from sex was part of the problem of both the men and the boys. Both were driven by a need for intimacy; all suffered from a sense of alienation.

One sex ring drafted a bill of rights for each of the boys involved. A key phrase was, "Every boy has a right to a loving relationship with at least one responsible male adult after whom he can pattern his life."[15] This suggests that the motivation for the boys involved is a close relationship with a father figure.

Robin Lloyd, in *For Money or Love,* tells of a man who took a thirteen-year-old boy into his home as a sexual companion. Eventually the man became the boy's guardian. The sex dropped out and was replaced by a father-son relationship. Once in a while, the man still sought sex from boys in a nearby town, but as he put it, "I have enough companionship at home to offset the need of seeking it elsewhere."[16]

It is very difficult to get those boys who have been the sexual partners of older men to testify against those men in court, especially if the boys have been well treated, given presents, taken on trips, and given love and affection. The boys themselves do not feel that they have been abused. For some, it is the first time in their lives that someone has treated them decently.

PART IV
Pornography,
Obscenity, and Prostitution

Chapter XIII
Kiddie Porn

In this day of sordid enterprises, child pornography surely reaches the depths of human depravity.[1]

—Senator Orrin Hatch, Utah

Less than 10 percent of the pornography market in the United States is devoted to sex with children.[2] It is aptly named kiddie porn, for some of the children used are as young as three years of age. Kiddie porn is an extremely lucrative business. The profits to be made from the sale of a fifty-foot reel of 8mm film, from a set of colored slides, from a video-tape cassette, or from books and magazines depicting children engaged in sexual activities, range anywhere from five to twenty-five times cost. Magazines retailing for $7.50 to $12.50 cost only thirty to fifty cents to produce. A pornographic home movie sells for up to $200.

Kiddie porn is a half-billion dollar a year business,[3] perpetrated to a large extent by independent amateurs. Anyone with a home movie camera or a Polaroid can go into business for himself, as did an aero-space engineer who wanted extra income. He placed an ad for eight- to fourteen-year-old girl models (with parental consent) for one-day photographic sessions. He was swamped by parents eager to put their children in front of the camera for the $200 fee he offered. When the police finally caught up with him, his sideline was earning him a quarter of a million dollars a year.[4]

Now that self-developing home movies are a reality, the amateur doesn't even have to worry about the film developer reporting him to the police. The supply of children is virtually unlimited, restricted only by one's ingenuity in recruiting them. Note the following examples:

In New Orleans, a Boy Scout troop was organized by a group of men for the purpose of producing pornographic films. The materials were sold nationwide. Three of the men involved behind the scenes were millionaires. The Scoutmaster of the troop was sentenced to seventy-five years in prison for his part in the case.[5]

A Colorado couple sold their twelve-year-old son for $5000 as a sexual companion to a wealthy Texan.[6]

A social worker in Illinois permitted his three foster sons to be filmed by a pornographer for $150 per child.[7]

A Los Angeles County grand jury indicted nine men on charges of operating an international child prostitution ring to make pornographic movies and to take pictures for smut magazines. The children involved ranged in age from six to twelve years, and were sold for sex at prices up to $1000. One of the men involved was the father of one of the children.[8]

In Tennessee, a boys' home for neglected children run by an Episcopal priest was used for filming homosexual orgies featuring the boys. Adult "sponsors" of the home could purchase the films or visit the home and engage in sex with the boy of their choice.[9]

In Chicago, a twenty-six-year-old foster father had sex with his fourteen-year-old foster son in front of a home movie camera. It was his intention to sell 2000 copies of the film for $50 each. He was caught when he turned the film over to an undercover policeman who said he could process the film with no questions asked.[10]

One enterprising porno ring used church and tax laws to their advantage. They set up a nonprofit "church" that in turn established camps and homes for wayward boys. The organization obtained funds from unwitting county, state, and federal agencies to pay for the boys' care. The children were made available to wealthy homosexuals for sexual purposes and were photographed for pornographic magazines and films. All of this with the tax-exempt blessing of the government until the law belatedly caught up with them.[11]

In Senate and House hearings on the sexual exploitation of children, the congressmen felt that they had established a connection between child prostitution and child pornography. The two topics, especially boy prostitution (see Chapter XV), were so intertwined in the hearings that it was difficult to separate one from the other. It did seem to be true that one source of children for the pornographic trade was boy prostitutes.

The green plastic garbage bags kept turning up monthly around Los Angeles for a year and a half. Inside were the dismembered, mutilated bodies of young boys, mostly Mexican. According to the testimony of a L.A. police officer, the boys were smuggled into this country to feed the kiddie porn industry. They were sold for $750 to $1500 to eager men who, it was speculated, obtained their sexual satisfaction from torturing boys.[12]

In Chicago, law enforcement officials uncovered a male prostitution ring that was to be set up on a national scale. Called the Delta Project, the plan was to establish "Delta Dorms" in large cities around the country. Each dorm would be run by an adult pedophile—the Delta Don—and would house four or five young boys, known as Delta Cadets. Sponsors were solicited through ads run in pornographic magazines catering to homosexuals. For a fee, the sponsors could either visit a dorm or arrange to have a cadet sent to his home. The ring was broken up before the plan could be implemented.[13]

In a quiet New Jersey township of 6000 people, a man and his wife lured eighteen teen-age girls into posing for nude photographs. Some were hitchhikers the man picked up, and others were enticed to his home to babysit for his two young girls. The couple used the photos to blackmail the girls into working as prostitutes for the man's friends, whom he invited to his rural home to "have some fun." An informer tipped off police, who investigated and charged the couple with maintaining a house of prostitution. None of the girls was charged with any crime because police saw them as innocent victims of the couple's brothel scheme.[14]

These cited vignettes are sufficient to give the reader an idea of the scope of the problem. They could easily be mutiplied many times over. It is difficult to convey to anyone who has not seen kiddie porn just what it is like. Adult bookstores all over the country offer over 264 different magazines featuring male and female children engaged in sexual behaviour. "Naughty Horny Imps," "Chicken Delight," "Child Discipline," "Boys Who Love Boys," or "Child Love"—the titles depict a frightening range of perversions. You can see in books or magazines or on film loops children deflowered on their communion day; children having sex with their daddies; children tortured and beaten; children masturbating; children raped or pictured in other sexual acts with adults, animals, other children, either their own or the opposite sex or with both sexes at once.

Among adults, kiddie porn involves four groups. The first is stimulated by it; the second makes a considerable profit from it; the third finds it turns their stomachs; and the fourth has never seen it. The last group may find these examples hard to believe.

Pornography is tailored to appeal to specific tastes and fantasies. Those who don't share those fantasies are usually unmoved by the pornography. Most people could look at transvestite pornography, for example, and fail to find anything erotic in it. But to the person with transvestite interests, it is very erotic; it captures his sexual fantasies. The same is true of bondage or sadomasochistic or homosexual pornography.

With child pornography, people who are not sexually stimulated by it are more than unmoved—they are actively repulsed by it. Perhaps it has to do with the often bewildered and unsmiling faces of the pictured children. They don't belong as participants in those activities. They should be out chasing a baseball, skipping rope, or cuddling a puppy. They should be doing anything but what they are doing. They are missing out on the normal activities of children growing up. When they become adults, they probably won't be able to enjoy adult activities, such as sex, either.

These child victims of pornography are being emotionally and spiritually murdered, according to Dr. Judianne Densen-Gerber, a New York psychiatrist and leader of the recent national campaign to eliminate child pornography.

"It's worse than homocide," says Sgt. Lloyd Martin of the Los Angeles Police Department's Sexually Exploited Child Unit. "A homicide is terrible, but it's over with very shortly. The victim of sexual exploitation has to live the rest of his or her life with those memories of what pornography and sexual deviation brings upon them."[15] Sergeant Martin estimates that 30,000 children pose for pornography in the Los Angeles area.

The Children

Who are these children who are the pint-sized stars of the porno trade? A substantial number of them are runaways. Their usual age is from ten to sixteen years. They have an average third grade reading level and no marketable skills. They escape to the big cities for a dream. Perhaps they run from abusive parents or an emotionally deprived home life. Some of them are victims of incest. Others are kids from well-off families who come to the city for a night or a weekend looking for excitement and adventure. They are runaways, too, from boredom and indifferent parents.

Many of them drift into being male or female hustlers on the city's streets. It isn't long before one of the "johns" asks to take some pictures or perhaps shoot a film. Other children are met at the bus or train depots of the cities by a smiling man who offers them a hot meal and a place to sleep. The kids who go with him may find themselves drugged, raped, and eventually turned out on the streets working for a pimp. They quickly learn how to turn a trick for $25 to $50. Before long, they, too, may meet someone with a camera.

A second source of children for pornographic purposes is parents. The beginning of this chapter gave a number of examples of how children are solicited. They range from the parents who sold their child to a wealthy homosexual to a prostitute who rented her three children to a pornographer. Or it may be a middle-class professional man and father who decides to make an extra income with his camera and the neighborhood children. Some parents are indifferent and don't care what happens to their children. For other parents, the lure of money is greater than their concern for their children.

There is reported to be an organization of parents interested in using children for sexual purposes. Sergeant Martin of the Los Angeles police testified before the House Committee on the Sexual Exploitation of Children that such an organization actually existed in Los Angeles and that it claimed 5000 members nationwide. Known as the René Guyon Society, it had for a slogan, "Sex before eight or then it's too late."[16]

Other parents advertise in sex magazines and underground newspapers.

Young couple who LOVE children seek other like-minded individuals with an interest in photography. We would like to hear from families and especially children who want to exchange films and pixs.

Amateur photographer seeks male models, 14–16, for nude photo sessions. I PAY well!

In an earlier age, Lewis Carroll *(Alice in Wonderland)* had a curious hobby—photographing young girls, six to twelve, in the nude. Four of his photos were recently exhibited for the first time at the Rosenbach Museum in Philadelphia. The photos supposedly were taken with the permission of the girls' mothers. Said a museum curator, "This is a very subtle issue...."[17] (Did he mean photographing nude children, getting the permission of the mothers, or exhibiting the photos?)

A third source of children for pornography is one that might easily involve your children or mine. It is simply any place where children congregate in groups. There is even money to be made in publications that inform adults where the children "hang out" in various cities around the country—the local "chicken house" or "pimple joint" as they are known in the trade. One such pamphlet, published in California and entitled, "Where the Young Ones Are," sold 70,000 copies at $5 per copy. It listed 378 places in fifty-nine cities and thirty-four states. Among the places suggested were: parks, arcades, drugstores, bowling alleys, quick food stores, discos, and beaches. It might be a summer camp, Boy Scout troop, church group, private school, or a children's home.

The congressional hearings unearthed publications that instructed adult readers how to infiltrate a boy's club and set up a sex and pornography ring. Another publication gave a step-by-step outline on how to pick up a child on a playground without getting caught. Kenneth Wooden, Director of the National Coalition of Children's Justice, testified before the House Committee about a letter made available by the Michigan State Police from a notorious chickenhawk (the young male victim is known in the trade as a "chicken," and the men who use boys, as "chickenhawks"). Written to other men, it gave explicit instructions on how to get into foster care or how to go after federal runaway money in order to get a "child of your own."

Chicago police found a newsletter for homosexuals being printed on the presses of the Cook County jail by a man waiting trial on charges of taking indecent liberties with ten teen-age boys. The man had advertised his newsletter services in gay publications and received replies from men all over the country.[18]

Not so many years ago, most of the child pornography in this country came from abroad—from Scandinavia, Germany, and Far Eastern countries such as Thailand. This has changed, and the United States is now a major producer—in cities like Chicago, New York, and Los Angeles.

Robin Lloyd tells an ironic tale in regard to the source of one bit of pornography. Working with the Los Angeles Police Department, Lloyd ordered a child pornography film from Denmark. When it arrived, the package bore an L.A. postmark. The police, working through the post office, located the distributor and raided his establishment. It came as a shock to Lloyd when the raid took place in the very apartment building next to his![19]

What happens to children who are used in pornography? Again, it is very difficult to make a general statement that is true for all children.

Some older children exploited through pornography drift into drugs and prostitution. There is some medical evidence that premature sexual intercourse can lead to increased risk of cervical cancer in females. But the major effects on children involved in pornography revolve around their self-esteem and the attitudes they develop toward others. Pornography involves a mechanical sex in which feelings are cut off from affection. The children come to view themselves as objects to be sold rather than as people who are important. They develop a bitterness toward the adults who required them to sell their bodies in order to receive adult affection. Some become cynical and exploitative in their sexual relationships and are unable to enjoy sex as adults. Some older children report feeling dirty and unwanted, and regret having missed out on a normal childhood. Of course, in kiddie porn, the child always receives a payment. It may be money, candy, a fix, or a trip to Disneyland, but it is there. Sex and relationships always have their price.

The Crusade against Kiddie Porn

In the summer of 1976, a package arrived at Odyssey House in New York City, headquarters of a nation-wide chain of drug rehabilitation centers for teen-agers. Inside was a kiddie porn magazine with a note calling attention to the existence of this kind of material. That was enough to start psychiatrist and founder of Odyssey House, Dr. Judianne Densen-Gerber, on a national crusade. She became, in her own words, "a raving banshee" over the issue of children being used in pornographic films and magazines. Dr. Densen-Gerber—a lawyer, mother, wife (of New York City's deputy chief medical examiner), and member of New York City's All Souls Unitarian Church—went on a national speaking tour. She showed films and gave talks on child pornography. She visited porno stores, bought their wares, and then held demonstrations outside the stores, exhibiting the materials. She collected kiddie porn from all over the world and then took her gleanings to Washington to testify at the hearing before the House Committee on Sexual Exploitation of Children.[20]

Dr. Densen-Gerber waved a magazine in front of the congressmen which had been purchased the previous week by her seventeen-year-old daughter, right there in the nation's capital. The magazine, discounted because the girl was under age, was called "Family Fucks,

The Families Who Fuck Together Stay Together." (Oddly enough, professionals do say one of the dynamics of incest is that it is a pathological attempt by family members to keep the family from splitting up.)

Dr. Densen-Gerber made a number of loose charges in her testimony that were difficult to document. One was the implication that organized crime was involved in child pornography. While that is a reasonable guess, there was little in either the Senate or House testimony to support such a statement. An article in *Time* stated that New York City's Mafia family had a large interest in the child pornography business, but it cited no sources for the statement.[21] It is generally believed that the Mafia has a major stake in adult bookstores around the country. To that extent, they distribute child pornography. But the production of kiddie porn still seems to be largely an amateur enterprise. Whether it remains that way or not, with its potential for tremendous profit, is another matter.

During her testimony, Dr. Densen-Gerber not only waved her magazines in front of the congressmen, she also rattled off the names of the magazines and read the blurbs on their covers (example: My Daddy taught me how to suck cock). Her frankness provoked a mild comment from Representative Railsback that she was conveying her message "maybe a little bit too sensationally." It provoked an even stronger rebuke from Pennsylvania's Representative Ertel. He thought that showing the titles and books before the TV cameras was counterproductive. His concern was that children would be watching the six o'clock news that evening and would have no way of selecting out what she had presented.

Dr. Densen-Gerber's reply: "So why don't you clean it up so I don't have any magazines to show? Why don't you worry less about me and more about the organized crime that is making these things?"

Mr. Ertel commented further that she could have presented the material in a written statement and not waved those magazines in front of the press.

During Densen-Gerber's crusade and the congressional hearing, kiddie porn disappeared almost entirely from the open market. It represents less than 10 percent of the total porno market and distributors were not going to jeopardize 90 percent of their income pushing kiddie porn while the heat was on.

Even on a recent visit to Times Square, I found no kiddie porn on open display. I expect it is still there under the counter, reserved for regular and known customers. There were some magazines featuring teen-agers, but the models looked over sixteen years of age. With their hair in pigtails, a pout on their faces, and a lollipop in their mouths, they resembled a caricature of a five-year-old teen-ager. A mail advertisement for pornography that I saw recently had a band across one corner of the cover that read, "All models over sixteen years of age."

Partly as a result of Dr. Densen-Gerber's crusade, early in 1978 Congress passed legislation against the sexual exploitation of children. The new law covered two areas. First, as a result of the supposed connection between child prostitution and pornography, that part of the U.S. Code known as the Mann Act was amended to prohibit the transportation of boys under sixteen across state lines for the purpose of prostitution. The Mann Act had previously applied only to females.

Secondly, the new law provided criminal penalties for persons convicted of sexual exploitation of children. Sexual exploitation was defined as producing a wide range of material involving the use of a minor (under sixteen) in actual or simulated sexual intercourse—oral, anal, or genital—between persons of the same or opposite sex; bestiality; masturbation; sadomasochistic abuse (for the purpose of sexual stimulation); and lewd exhibition of the genitals or pubic area of any person (one newspaper called it "public" areas!). Maximum penalties were fifteen years in prison and a fine of $15,000.

At nearly the same time as Congress acted, some states also passed similar legislation. Within four months of the passage of the law, two convictions by the U.S. District Court in Rhode Island were reported in the Boston *Globe*.[22] Both men were charged with violations of federal laws prohibiting shipping and distributing of kiddie porn films across state lines. One man was sentenced to three years in prison and fined $5000. The other was given what was described as the "maximum" five-year sentence. One could easily get the impression that the new law was producing results.

In fact, both men were sentenced under provisions of the old Federal Obscenity Laws (Chapter 71, Section 1465—Transportation of obscene matters for sale or distribution).[23] The first man pleaded guilty in November 1977, before the new law took effect. The second was also prosecuted under the old law, for he received a maximum sentence of five years. The maximum in the new law is fifteen years, but the old obscenity statute calls for a fine of not more than $5000 and imprisonment of not more than five years, or both.

All of which raises an interesting question: in view of these convictions under obscenity statutes, why was a new law needed? The new law made two changes. First, males were included under the Mann Act, a necessary addition to enable federal prosecution of those engaged in supplying boys for prostitution. Secondly, the thrust of the new legislation was the definition of kiddie porn as child abuse, rather than as obscenity. Congress has had problems in the past in attempting to outlaw pornography with people who cry "censorship" and claim violation of the First Amendment rights of free speech. The courts have had difficulty over the years in trying to define what obscenity and pornography are. (One judge admitted, "I can't tell you what it is, but I know it when I see it.")

Lawyers for the American Civil Liberties Union objected to the new law's inclusion of distributors, publishers, editors, and retailers.[24] Though the ACLU deplored the product, they felt the law violated the right of free speech. The ACLU condemned the sexual exploitation of children, but felt Congress should confine itself to going after the producers. Once child pornography was produced, the ACLU believed it was protected absolutely by the First Amendment. Much discussion ensued concerning limitation of the distribution of such material.

An original version of the House bill made only production illegal. The Senate tacked on distribution. The final version, sent to the White House for signature, contained penalties against both production and distribution. Whether the entire law may be unconstitutional or not is unclear. One can only wait for convictions under the law and see what happens in the courts. As for the extension of the Mann Act under the new law, there was little in either the House or Senate hearings to suggest that any significant number of males were being transported between states for the purposes of prostitution. The new law would only appear to have done something about a problem.

It would seem to be sensible to attack child pornography on the grounds that it is child abuse rather than on the murky grounds of obscenity. Most mental health professionals would agree that child sexual exploitation is child abuse.

Pornography and Sex Crimes

In her testimony before the House Committee, Dr. Densen-Gerber made the following charge. "The people who support and buy this kind of material are strengthening their pedophilic fantasies. Now when fantasies are stimulated, people go home and act out."

She was particularly concerned that pornography incited unacceptable behavior and gave people instructions on how to go about antisocial sexual acts. She exhibited examples of pornography which told parents how to have incest with their children; men how to pick up children in a park, molest them, and not be arrested; the joys of sexual gratification from beating the young; and how to penetrate a prepubescent girl who is not yet able, because of her smallness, to be penetrated in a standard missionary position. "This material produces sexual crimes against children," Dr. Densen-Gerber said.

About half of the American public would agree with Dr. Densen-Gerber in her conclusion that pornography leads to sex crimes. A survey of police chiefs found that nearly 60 percent believed that obscene books play a significant role in *causing* juvenile delinquency.[25] It is not uncommon to read in the newspaper about a rape or other sex crime in which the police found a stack of pornographic magazines and books in the suspect's apartment. The unstated implication is that the books "incited" the crime. Common sense would say that pornography can only encourage the activities it portrays. Sergeant Martin of the LAPD is quoted in the Washington *Star* as saying:

Every case [of child molesting] we've ever made out here, the guy's had this material. Take one man who picked up a five-year-old girl in the park. The guy had two briefcases containing ten rubber dolls, candy, a tube of Vaseline and a stack of books including *Lollitots, Moppets* and one called *Daddy Loves Little Girls.* [26]

Yet, in spite of this kind of evidence there are no definitive studies that demonstrate a cause and effect relationship between pornography and sex crimes. Surveys of mental health professionals show that large majorities believe that there are no harmful effects to adults from pornography.[27] It is not universally true that pornography produces sex crimes, or that when people's fantasies are stimulated, they go home and act out. Undoubtedly there are a few people for whom this is true, but for the majority of people it is not so. A case can be made for the view that pornography serves as a release valve for many people, reducing the tendency to act out. For people who are vulnerable, pornography can trigger undesirable behavior. But most people are not vulnerable, nor do they have such weak controls that pornography sends them rushing into the streets to commit sex crimes.

The Commission on Obscenity and Pornography, in their technical report volume, studied what happens when people are exposed to erotica. For some people, it led to an increase in masturbation or coital activity. For a smaller proportion of the people, this behavior was decreased by erotica. The majority of people reported no change in their sexual behavior at all. The Commission concluded that there is "no evidence that exposure to explicit sexual material plays a significant role in the causation of delinquency or criminal behavior among youth or adults."[28] The conclusion of another of the technical studies was that sexual deviance cannot be attributed to early sexual experience with erotica, nor did sex offenders differ from normal adults in the degree of their recent exposure to erotica.[29]

If one turns to sex offenders themselves, they report being less aroused by pornography than nonoffenders. For those sex offenders who were aroused, pornography led to increases in masturbation, while nonoffenders reported increases in heterosexual intercourse.

When sex offenders were asked directly if they thought there was a relationship between pornography and their sexual behavior, only 10 percent felt that there was.[30] This figure is surprisingly low. One would expect it to be higher since pornography becomes a convenient scapegoat for sex offenders to deny personal responsibility for their behavior.

An even more interesting research result is that sex offenders on the whole seem to have had less adolescent experience with erotica than other adults. For example, the age for sixty rapists when they first viewed pornography depicting heterosexual intercourse was 18.2 years, while for sixty matched nonsex offenders it was fifteen years. The rapists were on the average three years older before they saw depictions of heterosexual intercourse.[31] This suggests a generally deprived sexual environment with atypical and inadequate sexual socialization. Rather than being overexposed to sexual stimuli as children, they tended to be underexposed. Their early social environment was sexually repressed and deprived. There was usually a low family tolerance for nudity, an absence of sexual conversation in the home, and either punitive or indifferent parental responses to the child's sexual curiosity or interests. As adults, sex offenders continue to be sexually conservative, with rigid sexual attitudes and immature sexual/social relationships. (Remember the man who raped two boys, but thought consenting homosexual relations between adults was perverted?)

Could it be that sex offenders' crimes are related in some way to a *lack* of specific information about sex? The sexual behavior of child molesters is often child-like sex play with their victims. They are more comfortable relating to children than adults. While they may be repeating a childhood trauma with their victims, they may also be expressing a childish curiosity about sexual matters.

If pornography causes sex crimes one would expect that if restrictions on pornography were removed, there would be an upsurge in the incidence of sexual crimes. This has not been the case in Denmark, where the availability of explicit sexual materials has led to a decrease in the incidence of sexual crimes of all types.[32] Of particular interest is the fact that offenses against children in Denmark also dropped sharply. The 1969 figure was only 42.6 percent of the 1958–1969 average of these crimes.[33] This was during a time when porno was widely available in Denmark, and the year that the obscenity statute was formally repealed. Free access to pornography appeared to be related to a reduction in sex crimes.

The reason for this is not clear. Some people hypothesize a release valve phenomenon. We know that people learn from watching others and one form of vicarious learning is modeling—a demonstration of how to do something. It may be true that seeing one's fantasy modeled by others in pornography removes the need to do it oneself. Thus, pornography gives vicarious satisfaction to sexual impulses.

Others look to the forbidden fruit hypothesis. Things which are forbidden become more desirable, and one feels a greater pressure to do them because one is not supposed. to. When things become less secret, when prohibitions are removed, some of the motivation to act out is undercut.

Americans function on the premise that the best way to control impulses is to forbid them. In a simplistic manner, they reason that if certain behavior is undesirable, the thing to do is to pass a law against it. This thinking is at work in people who object to the removal of archaic laws concerning sexual behavior from the books. It is as if laws were necessary to provide an outside restraint on human impulses. Such people do not have strong enough inner controls to tell them not to do something; they need an external authority, the law in this case, to act as a brake on their impulses. They are like children looking to parents for direction.

Lawrence Kohlberg's research on morality showed that the majority of Americans function at this Stage Four "Law and Order" mentality. They are only comfortable when they know that good and bad are objectified in laws. Indeed, survey evidence shows that nearly half of American adults believe that pornography leads to moral breakdown.[34] So Congress passes a law that makes sexual exploitation of children a federal crime, punishable by prison and a fine. It amends the Mann Act to make interstate transportation of a boy for immoral purposes illegal.

However, passing laws is often only an illusion of doing something about a problem. It will not stop boy prostitution, and it will not stop the sexual exploitation of children in pornography. It is akin to a physician giving a pain-killer without ever finding out what is causing the pain. It treats symptoms and not causes.

The Senate Report for the Committee on the Judiciary put it very well:

> It should be emphasized that child pornography and prostitution are just individual aspects or symptoms of a larger context of social problems that confront the nation. Broken homes, alienated and runaway children, emotionally disturbed juveniles, alcohol and drug abuse among the very young, and widespread child abuse are among the national problems that help create the milieus in which child pornography can thrive.
>
> Against the backdrop of the breakdown of the family and the fundamental values of our society, questions must be asked regarding the adequacy of our educational system, the effectiveness of our social agencies, our ability to deal with poverty and unemployment, and the quality of our justice system. Child pornography and prostitution are deadly serious problems. But even more menacing is the fact that these are only tips of an iceberg.[35]

Chapter XIV
Violence—The Ultimate Obscenity

In the Senate hearings on violence and obscenity, Senator Hatch expressed the view that "child pornography surely reaches the depths of human depravity." Gloria Steinem, in an editorial in *Ms.*, stated her opinion that child pornography was neither sexual nor a perversion. It is rather, she wrote, the obscene use of power.[1] Perhaps it is misuse of power rather than child pornography which is the ultimate obscenity.

Of course, it is males who are guilty of this obscenity. It is men who make, buy, and use pornography, especially the white, married, middle-class, middle-aged male. Women rarely buy pornography and are seldom seen inside of porno bookstores (if they are it is usually to buy rubber products). If they are involved at all in producing pornography that sexually exploits children, it is usually through their involvement with a man.

Pornography is tailored to the male psyche, to reflect male fantasies. While the content is sexual, according to Steinem, pornography meets a male need for superiority and power and gives males permission to be violent through sexual conquest.

A similar view is expressed by Phyllis Chesler in her book *About Men.* "Pornographic fantasies," says Dr. Chesler, "allow men freedom from guilt about their real or repressed sadism."[2] Indeed, her conversations with men about their sexual fantasies would appear to bear out her observation about sadism. Men described rape fantasies, scenes of gang rapes and mutilation, seduction and strangling, and "clever" or omnipotent sexual control of extremely young and innocent children. It is precisely these sadistic fantasies that are found in most pornography.

123

The most common sexual fantasy in pornography is one in which men sadistically dominate women or children sexually. The reverse scenario, in which women sadistically dominate men, is produced for transvestite men. It is the humiliation of the male being treated as the devalued female which leads to erotic arousal for them. Such pornography does not appeal to women, for they find it difficult if not impossible to be sexually aroused by fantasizing sadistic sexual aggression toward men.

Nor does sadistic sexual aggression toward a man by other men appeal to women. Such porno is directed to certain homosexuals who are erotically aroused by being dominated by a strong man. Most heterosexual men would find pornography in which a male is the object of sadistic sexual aggression by other men arousing, but the emotion aroused would be anxiety, not sexuality. The anxiety stems from being placed in the devalued female role.

Women, too, have fantasies in which they are sadistically dominated by men. It is important to stress that these are fantasies, and not a wish for a reality experience. Men would like to believe that all women wish to be raped. They confuse male pornography with women's psyches. The rape fantasy for women helps relieve guilt about their real or repressed masochism. It also allows women to vicariously experience sexual aggression by identifying with the male in their fantasy. Power through sexual domination is largely a male monopoly.

Chesler makes two other points about the function of pornographic sexual fantasies for men. By identifying with sexually active and satisfied men in pornographic fantasies, a male is able to deny his passive feelings, fears, concerns about sexual inadequacy, sexual fatigue or awkwardness, or his flagging sexual interest due to sexual aging. Perhaps in this latter, Chesler touches upon one aspect of the dynamics of sex between men and boys.

The older man who seeks sex with young boys may be attempting to reassure himself that he is still potent and capable of competing sexually with younger men. The competition may be with his own lost adolescent sexual potency, or with his own son. Some men in middle age, who have a son approaching adolescence, develop an erotic interest in young boys and act upon it. Mixed in with the competition may be a disguised search for the tenderness men yearn for but were never allowed to experience with their own fathers. By also identifying with the boy, the man experiences a vicarious satisfaction of that wish.

Chesler's second point is that male pornographic sexual fantasies are a way of denying, absorbing, or containing male violence toward other men. Male sexual aggression upon the bodies of women allows men to associate with other men without danger of male aggression against them. Andrea Dworkin puts it more directly: "Women absorb male aggression sexually so that men are safe from each other."[3] United in the belief that every man is superior to all women in every way, as demonstrated by their power to sexually dominate women, men are spared the necessity of annihilating each other more often than they do. Women are sexual sponges for male hostility.

Chesler also makes the observation that pornographic sexual fantasies ward off submerged, reactive, and rejected desires for heterosexual incest or intimacy. Few male fantasies involve older women. They usually involve female sex objects much younger than themselves. If Chesler is correct, a potential motivation for the choice of young children as sexual objects may be an extreme reaction against a male committing psychic incest with his mother.

Chesler's remarks are addressed to adult pornography and she does not touch upon kiddie porn. Few writers, however, pay much attention to the possible sadistic elements involved in the sexual exploitation of children. People are horrified by the sexual behavior, and focus their attention upon that. Perhaps the aggressive and sadistic aspects should receive more careful scrutiny. Children are the epitome of the helpless, weak, innocent, and powerless victim. Stressing the sadistic aspect of the sexual exploitation of children helps it to be recognized as closely related to other forms of child abuse, such as child battering. The similarity lies in the common thread of anger, hostility, and violence directed against children by men, and perhaps indirectly at the women who are mothers to those children. It highlights the American male's ambivalent attitudes toward children.

Dr. Densen-Gerber is quoted in an article as asking the question, "Do we hate our children?" She believes that America does, perhaps not as individuals, but that our institutions certainly do. "The system hates children," she says.[4]

I would agree with her conclusion. As a society, we are ambivalent about children, as demonstrated by the consistency with which children end up at the bottom of the list of national priorities. The locus of the problem of violence toward children is an intrapsychic conflict in adults, primarily in males. It is related to the male's inability to tolerate dependency; to distorted ideas of masculinity; to failure to resolve competition, rivalry, and jealousy with fathers, and then to transfer that conflict onto their relationships with their own sons; to the need to be powerful, competent, and in control; and to the tendency to maintain their own egos by continually reasserting their superiority over women and children.

Looked at from this point of view, it becomes logical to ask, "Why is the pornographic exploitation of children abuse, but the pornographic exploitation of adults obscenity?" It, too, is a form of abuse. Why single out children for protection, and then leave them on their own once they reach sixteen years of age? Pornography involving adults is part of the broad spectrum Steinem calls "the physical and psychic violence done by one human being to another."[5]

As women's liberation becomes more of a reality, perhaps we will see more violence perpetrated by women. Some women mistakenly assume that liberation means becoming like men. That would indeed be a tragic mistake. Equality is not the same as progress.

Violence in TV and Movies

One of the concerns of the House and Senate hearings on the sexual exploitation of children was what the effect of a law would be on legitimate film producers. Would they be prohibited from making any film which contained even a single scene that involved a child in sexual behavior? The popular film *The Exorcist* was cited as an example. That film contained a brief scene in which a minor simulated masturbation. In the opinion of some, legitimate films involve the issue of "freedom of speech" and have to be judged under the applicable obscenity laws. That would require a determination of whether the movie as a whole was obscene, that is, appealed mainly to prurient interests and intended to stimulate the viewer sexually. Such films would probably not be judged obscene in their entirety.

A more difficult question involves a movie such as *Pretty Baby,* a film about a child prostitute. Some critics raise the disturbing question of whether this movie isn't a form of sexual exploitation of children. Money is being made by a movie company about the sexual behavior of a child. What makes such a film different from hard-core porno? Some people would call the movie obscene.

These are not easy questions for our society to answer. C. Henry Kempe, the pioneer author in the child abuse field, raised a slightly different question about the film. His concern was not that the film would corrupt the audience, but rather that there would be deleterious effects on the child actress who performed in the role.

"The fact that young Brooke Shields insists that she is just fine means nothing," Dr. Kempe said in a letter to the editor of the Boston *Globe*. "It simply is not up to a twelve-year-old to make some decisions."[6]

Dr. Kempe feels the film sets a bad precedent. In his opinion, the parents of other child actors participating in child pornography are now "home free." Why should they stop at using a twelve-year-old actress? Now they can try age six, he wrote.

Dr. Kempe says, "The sexual exploitation of anyone, even child actors, is a crime in all of our states." While he understood the public's rights under the first amendment to see the film once it was made, he failed to understand how the film could have been legally made in the first place.

In another letter to the editor, a woman gave her views of the effects on children of seeing the movie *Saturday Night Fever*.

"This is no movie for the young. . . . What they see . . . [is] an unceasing storm of physical violence, verbal violence, and sexual violence. I believe there is such a thing as psychological child abuse, and letting children learn about sex by watching a Brooklyn gang rape must certainly be labeled as such."[7]

This woman put her finger on the problem exactly. The majority of people, when they think of obscenity, think of sexual material. The real villain may not be sex, but violent sex, and ultimately, just plain violence. We carefully guard our children from sexual material, but we expose them to an unchecked flood of violence on TV and in the movies. Are we not perpetuating the male myth of sexual violence? We are just beginning to wake up to the violent content of much TV fare aimed at children, not to mention the prime time violence that we naively assume they don't see because they are all tucked safely in bed having nightmares.

The dawning awareness of TV violence is having one interesting consequence—disturbing social questions are getting dropped into the laps of judges. Unfortunately, this is probably the wrong place for them to be.

The recent TV movie *Born Innocent* raised some dilemmas for NBC when it first came out in 1974. In that film, a teen-age girl is raped in the shower of a detention home by four other female inmates using the handle of a plumber's helper.

Four days after the movie was shown on KRON in San Francisco, three girls—eleven, fourteen and fifteen—raped a nine-year-old girl on a San Francisco beach with a beer bottle. A fifteen-year-old boy stood watch while the rape went on.

The victim's mother filed an $11 million damage suit for negligence against NBC and the owners of KRON, charging that the television drama had inspired the attack on her daughter. Her lawyer insisted that NBC was negligent and reckless in airing the show at 8:00 P.M., an hour when adolescents might be watching and possibly pick up the idea of imitating such a sexual assault.

The California Medical Association filed an amicus curiae on behalf of the child, stating, "The health and welfare of our society demands that broadcasters be accountable for their programming."[8]

The case went to trial in San Francisco in August 1978. NBC attorneys argued that the issue to be proven was "incitement," one of the rare and small exceptions to the First Amendment. A superior court judge ruled that the plaintiff must prove that NBC incited the attack on the girl. Bringing the case under the First Amendment protection to freedom of expression placed a heavy burden of proof on the plaintiffs, who would have had to prove that NBC tried to incite a rape when it televised the show. Consequently the case was dismissed.

The issue of responsibility remains open for our society. This was not the first time that TV had been indicted for playing a role in promoting violence in real life. A number of years ago, youths in Boston poured gasoline on a victim and set him afire, duplicating an incident from a TV crime show.

More often it has been the perpetrators of crimes who claimed that they were influenced by TV. A fifteen-year-old youth convicted of murdering his eighty-three-year-old neighbor, unsuccessfully used the defense at his trial that he was a victim of "involuntary television intoxication." Sentenced to life imprisonment, the youth recently had a $25 million damage suit filed on his behalf.[9]

It is unlikely that there is a simple cause and effect relationship between TV and real-life violence. Studies have shown that exposure to violence on TV does raise children's thresholds of violence in real life. But it is the vulnerable child or adult who imitates the violence he sees on TV.

Children who imitate an aggressive rape scene from TV are already children in trouble, with problems handling their sexual/aggressive feelings. TV is not the cause of this violence—however it may in some cases be the trigger. The overwhelming majority of people are not impelled to commit acts similar to what they see on TV. It is an open question as to whether there may be more subtle undesirable effects on adults and children from watching TV. TV, like much else in our culture, needs to be examined more closely.

Incest and Violence

While incest may not involve the direct use of physical force and violence, it seems to be surrounded by a past and present aura of violence.

One study of sixteen juvenile offenders who were incest victims linked the incest with a tendency to commit crimes against human life. There were five cases of attempted suicide among the children, and also two threats of murder related to the incest.[10]

In another study of fourteen child victims of incest, the authors described the family/marital situation and characterized over half of them as involving frequent violence. The incest took place in a home situation that exposed the child to violent scenes, and either the child or mother lived in fear of the father. The threat of violence may be another pressure forcing the child into complying with the incest. This same study revealed over half the men involved abused alcohol, and one father abused drugs. It also documented violent sequels to incest. Two fathers attempted suicide; a mother was murdered by her son; one child was raped by an uncle; and another was sexually molested.[11]

Sgroi cautions about potential violent reactions in the family when a child sexual assault situation is exposed. In her opinion, these situations are exceedingly volatile. She puts forth an interesting hypothesis, namely that the coming to light of a previously undiscovered incest may underlie the puzzling cases of family mass murders, those in which the father slays his spouse, all the children, and then commits suicide.[12]

A further link between incest and violence has turned up in the work of agencies who treat offenders and victims. The Center for Rape Concern in Philadelphia reports that 50 percent of the offenders they have seen were sexually abused as children. Groth reports that 30 percent of the 200 committed child offenders he studied reported sex assaults as children, in contrast with only 3 percent in a control group of police officers.[13] Other studies report that the mothers of incest victims have often been sexually assaulted themselves as children.

Eroticized Hatred

I have stressed throughout this book that adults reenact childhood sexual traumas in an attempt to undo the trauma and lessen and master the anxiety originally associated with it. I have sometimes called this process by the psychoanalytic name—repetition compulsion.

One might ask why repetition of the trauma never seems to lead to mastery. After molesting a number of children, why don't molesters stop and progress to more normal sexual behavior and practices?

The only satisfactory answer to that question that I have found is in a book by Stoller, *Perversion, the Erotic Form of Hatred.* Stoller throws out the concept of repetition compulsion and takes a different tack.

He writes about sexual aberration(s) as erotic technique(s) that one uses as one's complete sexual act, and that differs from culture's traditional definition of normality. Sexual aberrations are of two kinds—variants (deviations) and perversions.

It is the perversions that are of interest here. A perversion, according to Stoller, depends upon one's attitude toward the object. If it is to harm the object and is sensed as an act of revenge, then it is a perversion. The key to perversion is hostility.

A perversion is a fantasy—usually acted out but sometimes restricted to a daydream—primarily motivated by hostility. The fantasy is one of revenge and is hidden in the actions that make up the perversion. This fantasy converts a childhood trauma into an adult triumph.

Stoller believes that the trauma of childhood, memorialized in the details of the perversion, is a reliving of an actual historical sexual trauma. This trauma was aimed either at the child's anatomical state (sex) or gender identity (masculinity/femininity). In the perverse act, trauma is turned into pleasure, orgasm, and victory.

Thus, in a perversion, one repeats the trauma because in repetition one is now able to escape the old trauma and achieve revenge and orgasm. (Often the escape is accomplished by making someone else the victim.) Repetition comes about because escape, revenge, and orgasm deserve repeating. The reduction of anxiety and the reward of pleasure from revenge and orgasm reinforce the complex behavior that make up the perversion.

Stoller goes on to say that any time there is too much stimulation, too little discharge, or severe guilt in the child, these will be sensed as traumatic and will need to be transformed into triumph via the magic of the perverse ritual. (Too much pleasure and too little guilt, on the other hand, result in a deviation. The deviant aberration, in contrast to the perverse aberration, does not primarily involve the staging of forbidden fantasies, especially the fantasy of harming others. Instead, it involves holding on to a deviant way of getting pleasure.)

Stoller's views take us in two directions. From the viewpoint of the child, it is the element of hostility against him that causes the psychic distress and may lead to a future perversion. From the viewpoint of the offender, each act against a child plays out a hostile fantasy of revenge against an adult of the past. To understand his behavior, we should look for the hostile element and for the trauma of childhood that he is reenacting. We must understand this in order to treat the offender.

While I have focused here on sexual abuse, remember also that the violence in physical abuse, which is even more blatant, has a similar damaging effect on the child's development and is linked to future adult violence. A survey of Auburn, New York, State Prison inmates, all of whom were incarcerated for violent crimes, revealed that 95 percent of them had been abused as children.[14]

Perhaps, after all, violence is the ultimate obscenity.

Chapter XV
Child Prostitution

The world's oldest profession has had an influx of new blood. A rapidly growing trend in the United States is for young teen-age girls to go into prostitution. New York City police estimate that a large proportion of the 20,000 runaway children in the city are available for commercial sex. Rings of girl prostitutes, some as young as twelve years of age, work Chicago, earning up to $200 a night.[1] Los Angeles, Houston, Boston, San Francisco, and other large cities can tell similar stories.

Recently there has been a change in the pattern, however. Whereas teenage prostitution has always been present in the large cities, now it has spread to smaller cities and towns, in the Midwest, in New England, and in southern border states like Kentucky. New York City has the reputation as a pipeline for young prostitutes, drawing runaway children to that city like a magnet. A New York State Select Committee on Crime heard evidence that one source of children was, of all places, Minneapolis, Minnesota. According to the testimony of a Minneapolis police officer, 300 to 400 children a year arrive from that city to end up selling sex on the streets of New York.[2]

Behind the teen-age victims are as many as 800 pimps, men who live off the earnings of their girls. Those earnings are considerable. One girl collected $100,000 for her pimp while she ended up with only $800. Another fourteen-year-old girl collected $4000 in ten weeks for her pimp. There is evidence, too, that the Mafia is moving back into prostitution, turning the clock back to the 1930s. The topless/bottomless bars and massage parlors owned by the mob are recruiting centers for young female prostitutes. The mobsters may also own many of the hotels where the prostitutes' "marks" can rent rooms for a few hours of sex.[3] Pimps who break the girls in can sell them to other pimps for prices up to a thousand dollars.

The girls who don't bring in the money or who try to escape from their pimps are subjected to brutal beatings to keep them in line. The girls are usually runaways, fleeing alcoholic, drug-addicted, brutal, or abusive parents. Many have been victims of incest in their own homes. It is estimated that 75 percent of adolescent prostitutes have been involved in incestuous relationships while 22 percent of 200 adult prostitutes in Seattle, Washington, had been incestuously molested.[4]

The girls willingly leave the small towns and cities with their pimps to go to New York City. Their relationship with their pimps is a strange one indeed. In spite of the abusive treatment they receive, they accept their pimp as a kind of father image. Forced into degradation, stripped of their self-esteem, and brutally treated, they still remain loyal to their pimps. The bond may be one of fear of what will happen to them if they try to leave, but it is strong nonetheless. Prosecution of pimps often fails because the girls will not testify against them.

Police efforts to crack down on pimps have not been successful. Charging them with felony crimes such as "soliciting for a juvenile prostitute" has not deterred them. Some states have opted for jail sentences for all convicted pimps, prostitutes, and their "johns." One police officer suggested that the men who patronize the teen-age prostitutes don't need jail sentences. He suggested that their names be published in the local newspapers instead.

In an unusual case early in 1978 in New York, a customer who sodomized a fourteen-year-old prostitute for $10 in a Times Square hotel brought prostitution charges against the girl after she and three other persons robbed him. The case was dismissed by a female family court judge, who ruled that sex for a fee was recreational and not a crime. Arguing that adult prostitution laws were unconstitutional and that prostitution did not harm the public health, safety, or welfare, the judge further reasoned that since the child's act would therefore not be a crime if committed by an adult, under state law it was not an act of juvenile delinquency.

As could certainly be predicted, the judge's decision caused a public furor. A minister who runs a youth shelter for runaways in Times Square called the decision "immoral, outrageous and unbelievable." The city decided to appeal the judge's decision, and Mayor Koch said the state could not look aside when a fourteen-year-old girl "decides she is going to sell her body."[5]

The judge sharply rapped police who she said took the attitude that the women who supply sex are immoral, but the men who patronize them are blameless. She pointed out that of over 3000 persons arrested in prostitution cases in six months of the prior year, less than 2 percent were customers.[6] In fact, the man who brought the charges against the girl in this case was not charged either with patronizing a prostitute or statutory rape.

If nothing else, the judge's decision focused attention on the sex bias in prostitution laws in this country. The case also pointed out the inconsistencies in applying the laws. The female prostitute in this case was also, under New York State law, a victim of statutory rape. She could not legally give her consent to sexual behavior.

The principle that a behavior is not juvenile delinquency if the same crime were committed by an adult is a reasonable one. However, this principle was developed in quite a different context. It corrected a long-standing abuse in the treatment of juveniles who, for years, could be given sentences—reform school or foster homes—far in excess of any sentence given to an adult who committed a similar offense. Originating in the Supreme Court's Gault decision, in other cases involving due process for children committed to mental institutions, and in cases involving the rights of school children to free expression of their ideas, the thrust of the law has been to grant children the same procedural safeguards in court as granted to adults.[7]

The application of the principle that what is not a crime for an adult is not a crime for a child, puts the issue of the rights of children versus the need to protect children squarely on the line. Prostitution among adults may be a victimless crime, but is that true when the prostitute is a child? Do not the rights of the child, who is to be treated before the law as an adult, conflict in this case with the state's interest in protecting the health, safety, and welfare of children?

The case points up our confused and ambivalent thinking about both prostitution and the welfare of children. What is needed is a rethinking of our societal values and a vehicle for resolving the increasing "rights" conflicts that are more common these days. In our myopia we don't realize that tampering with the social system in one area to correct inequalities can throw the system out of kilter in other areas. On the one hand, we say the child is a victim, and on the other, we attempt to prosecute her. Note in this case, no attempt was made to prosecute the property crime against the victim, that is, robbery. The child was charged with prostitution, not robbery. One can't help but wonder if King Solomon would have solved this dilemma with the same facility he showed the two women who both claimed to be the mother of the same child. The attitudes of our society already seem to be split in half. The question is how can we put the pieces back together to make a coherent whole?

Boy Prostitution

The usual notion about sexual contact with male children is that these are sexual assaults in which the victim is anally raped or forced to perform oral sex acts. In most cases, this is not so. There may be up to 300,000 young boys between the ages of eight and seventeen in this country who make a business of selling themselves for sex to male adults.[8] The majority of these boys are runaways. They can be found congregating on street corners in certain sections of most any large city. In tight jeans and T-shirts, they lounge around on display to the men in cars that slowly cruise up and down the street. A car stops, and a boy detaches himself from the group and strolls over to the car. Leaning in the window, he carries on a short conversation with the driver. Once convinced that the man is not an undercover cop, he opens the door and slips inside. The car drives off. In a short time the boy is back on the street, anywhere from $20 to $50 richer. Four times a night, seven nights a week can mean an impressive amount of money. A twelve-year-old boy in Los Angeles can earn $1000 a day in prostitution.[9]

For many boys, a good hunk of that money may disappear to support a drug habit. One reporter of the boy prostitution scene in New York City noted that young male prostitutes on 42nd Street outnumbered the female prostitutes five to one.[10]

Each year in America some 1 million children, many of them teenagers, run away from home. A considerable number of them, both male and female, support themselves on the streets by selling the only thing they have to sell—their bodies. As one policeman put it, to survive these kids either "drop their pants or pull up their skirts."[11]

The boy prostitutes more or less willingly engage in sex with men. They are often the initiators of the sexual contact and there is no shortage of men to buy what they have to sell. Rarely will the chicken-hawk resort to force, conversion, violence, or rape to get sex. There is no need. The supply of young boys is more than adequate. The entire transaction is strictly a business deal. Rossman estimates that the number of criminally promiscuous chickenhawks in the United States may be as many as 50,000.[12]

The majority of these contacts involve oral sex or masturbation. Anal intercourse is fairly rare and usually costs extra. One study suggested that anal intercourse occurred in only about 4 percent of all cases of man-boy contacts.[13]

One might wonder what the boys think of the sexual activities in which they engage. Do they, for example, consider themselves homosexually oriented? By and large, the boys see themselves as heterosexual. They use sex to exploit the adults who want what they have. Their sexual activities with men are a way of making money. Runaways need the money to live, and sex is simply an easy way to get it without having to work.

In a curious bit of rationalization, the boys distinguish between being active or passive as a basis for deciding if an act is homosexual or not. Letting the men blow them (perform fellatio) is not uncommon and is not considered a homosexual act by the boys. If they did it to the man, then they would be "queer." Many of the boys refuse to take the active role in this practice. By not doing so, they maintain their self-image of normality. In this, as in many things, money could change their minds, but even then, they would be doing it for the money, not because they wanted to or enjoyed it. As one boy put it: "But remember one thing . . . I was the one getting blown. I never did it to the queer. . . . Anyway, I always closed my eyes when the queer worked on me, and I imagined it was a girl that was doing it to me."[14] Like the little child who believes it is all right to tell a lie if you have your fingers crossed, so the heterosexual fantasy of the boy prostitute keeps the act from being homosexual in his mind.

The street hustler is likely to be a boy of lower-class origins. The middle- or upper-class boy who gets involved in prostitution may turn to hitchhiking rather than street hustling. In smaller towns, he may hang out in the bus depot, the YMCA, or the public toilets in the park. In his case, money may not be the major motivation. It may be boredom or an act of aggression against indifferent parents.

Some people point out that the runaway boy prostitute may engage in sex not only for the money, but also because he is seeking love, affection, and friendship. They point out how often these boys come from fatherless homes, or homes in which the father is cruel or abusive. They suggest the search for a loving father-figure is a motivation, even though the context is a business transaction.

Others suggest many boys get into prostitution out of a sense of boredom and a desire for adventure. Bombarded with sexuality in the media, unable to find acceptable sexual relationships with girls, they turn to temporary sexual relationships with men. These are not love relationships, but strictly pleasure and excitement adventures. In a society that doesn't allow adolescents to work or to have legal sex with teen-age girls, or doesn't do much to challenge their interests, boys quickly become bored and turn to sex for pleasure.

Of course, there is a certain amount of sexual desire and release that comes from the contacts. At around seventeen years of age, teen-agers are sexually active and at the peak of their sexual lives in terms of frequency of response and rapidity of recovery. Yet teen-agers are not allowed or encouraged to have regular heterosexual relation-ships. Our society's unrealistic attitudes toward teen-agers having a realistic sex life help to create and maintain a willing supply of boy prostitutes. Strangely enough, when an outraged community discovers what is going on, and the police become active in driving boy prostitutes off the streets, the problem increases rather than decreases. Decreasing the supply of available boys only drives up the price. The increased lucrativeness attracts more boys into prostitution, and before long the "meat racks" of the city are once again restocked.

There is nothing to support the notion that boy prostitutes grow up to become homosexuals. A survey of 300 male prostitutes known to the Danish police found the great majority were heterosexual and remained so even after years of experience in prostitution. Only 15 percent were true homosexuals or bisexuals. The majority grew away from the homosexual milieu as they grew older.[15] Many end up mar-rying in their late teens. The life of a boy on the streets is quite short. By his late teens or early twenties, he is no longer desired as a sex partner. The chickenhawks are looking for younger prey. What once he sold, he may now have to give away. Some may become chicken-hawks themselves in time and end up buying what once they sold.

In an excellent article on the boy prostitution scene in Boston, Philip Harris has written about the differences between male and female hustling.[16] First, there is not the exploitation in male hustling that exists in female prostitution. Pimping is rare among males. Second, you don't see the commercialization of male sex that is familiar in the female side of the sex for sale business (the strip joints, peep shows, B-girls, porno shops, and the sex circus of a Times Square). Third, you don't find the boisterous, rowdy behavior of the patrons in gay bars in the male hustling area that you find in the female prostitution areas of the city. Violence is rare in male sex encounters, quite unlike the female sex scene.

Harris presents some sharp vignettes of the young males who become hustlers on Boston's streets. Some are homosexuals trying to come out; others consider themselves bisexual; still others insist they are straight and are only having sex with males for the money. ("Hey, if some guy wants to give you twenty bucks to let him suck your cock. . . .")

The boys range from twelve to twenty-five years of age, from elementary school dropouts to college graduates. Many, but not all, come from broken homes. Harris concludes: "For many kids hustling is just plain not so bad. It's good money. It's a way to stay alive. It's friends and sex. And in a drab world of humdrum workaday life that the hustler can't accept, it's excitement and glitter and escape."

PART V
Deviant Sexual Environments

Chapter XVI
The Cases of Two Males

Because of the vulnerability of children and their dependency upon adults, almost any form of adult-child sexual behavior is considered abusive. When concerned adults intervene in such relationships, their attention usually focuses upon the sexual behavior. Every effort is made to separate the child from the adult, who is usually seen as the sexual aggressor. There may be some concern with punishing the adult, or even some psychiatric help for the child to alleviate the supposed trauma, but the problem is rarely conceptualized in broader terms. Often the assumption is made that once the child has been separated from the adult, the problem is solved. The failure to recognize the broader implications of sexual abuse means that these children do not receive the help they desperately need.

Sexual abuse is usually only one symptom that a child is in psychological trouble. While sexual abuse may indicate a disturbance in the child's sexual development, often it does not. However, sexual abuse always indicates a primary disturbance in the child's emotional relationships with adults. Usually, deviant patterns of relating develop in which sexual behavior satisfies nonsexual needs of the child.

Sexual abuse usually occurs in the broader context of a disturbed psychosocial environment. Adults who have failed to protect the child from sexual abuse may also have failed to protect the child in other areas. It is common, for example, to find that a sexually abused child lives in a deprived environment. There is always emotional deprivation, and sometimes physical deprivation and neglect as well. In the case of foster children who have been sexually abused, there is often, in addition to deprivation, a high incidence of violence within their families. Often, the sexually abused children or their siblings have been battered or have witnessed much physical violence between their parents. The consequences of emotional and physical deprivation, as well as the over-exposure to violence and sexuality, are far more harmful to the child's personality development than is the sexual abuse per se.

The sexual abuse itself often stirs up feelings of guilt, fear, and anxiety in the child. These feelings may be expressed as disturbed behavior in areas quite unrelated to sexual behavior, as for example, in learning difficulties in school, nightmares, bed wetting, or aggressive behavior toward others. The disturbed behaviors are symptoms of general distress.

Thus, intervention, if it is to help the child, must explore the child's total environmental adjustment. Special attention must be paid to what factors allowed the sexual abuse to happen, what nonsexual needs the behavior met in the child, and in what ways the child's emotional relationships with adults are disturbed. The following case demonstrates how an incident of sexual abuse fitted into a child's total environment and created difficulties for the child in other areas.[1]

Mark

Mark was eight and a half when he was admitted to a child care center from the foster home where he had been living for over a year. His foster mother had become increasingly incapable of dealing with Mark's aggressive behavior toward other children and his nightly bed wetting.

The child care staff at the center observed that Mark showed many signs of disturbed behavior. He wet his bed every night, sucked his thumb constantly, and was preoccupied with sexual activity and stimulation. He masturbated frequently and crawled into bed at night with the younger boys and tried to initiate sex play. When the staff supervised his nighttime behavior more closely, they reported with considerable agitation that Mark turned his sexual attention upon the cottage pet, a mongrel dog.

Mark's case record revealed that he and his four siblings originally came into foster care because of severe emotional and physical neglect. They were the natural children of two immature and inadequate people. Both parents had been deprived and neglected themselves as children. The father was a sporadic alcoholic and the mother had been in a mental hospital. She had many physical complaints and used these as

an excuse to stay in bed much of the time. The home environment was
chaotic. The children often went without food and adequate clothing.
They slept on urine-soaked mattresses and lived amid incredible filth.
The children witnessed frequent verbal and physical fights between
the parents and were left on their own for days while the parents were
out drinking.

In the course of investigating the home situation prior to moving
the children into foster care, it was discovered that a frequent visitor
to the home was a retarded uncle in his twenties. This uncle was well
known to the local police for sexually molesting children and dogs.
The uncle frequently slept at Mark's house, and when he did, he shared
a bed with one or more of the children. This practice was allowed
in spite of the fact that both parents were well-aware of the uncle's
deviant sexual behavior.

When the social worker asked if the uncle may have molested
Mark, the father just shrugged his shoulders and said, "Kids have to
learn about that stuff sooner or later." The mother, on the other hand,
vehemently denied that Mark had been singled out for molestation and
said, "He [the uncle] has sex with all the kids." The mother herself
frequently took all the children to bed with her, not for sexual reasons
but to ward off her sense of loneliness and isolation.

Commentary   The first obvious deviation in Mark's psychosocial
environment is the failure of the parents to protect him from the sexual
abuse of the uncle. The lesson in relationships that Mark and other
children learn from this parental failure is that you can't trust adults
to protect you. Mark's basic lack of trust in adults, greatly augmented
by the parents' failure to physically care for and nurture him, will be
an obstacle to the efforts of other adults to help him in the future.

A second point that Mark's case dramatically makes is that child
victims are often susceptible to adult seduction because of severe
emotional deprivation in the home environment. Rarely, if ever, does
sexual behavior in a young child have a sexual motivation. To understand the sexual behavior of a child, one must look more closely at
the child's nonsexual needs. It is often found that sexually abused
children were engaged at the time in affection-seeking behavior in their
relationship with the adult. (In foster children with severe emotional
deprivation, this need for affection may be an even stronger motivation
than usual.) Satisfaction of the childhood need for love and affection

provided by the sexual encounter reinforces a deviant childhood pattern of obtaining affection through sexual behavior.

A third pattern that the environment encourages when it allows children to be victimized is that, in the absence of parent protection, the child often defends himself by identifying with the aggressor. In his current behavior in foster care, Mark repeats the trauma that happened to him—with one difference. Instead of being the victim, Mark has now become the aggressor, like his uncle, and seeks out defenseless children and dogs to molest.

Mark's Development   After nearly four years of foster care, Mark's difficulties in relating to others became clearer. He showed a continuing preoccupation with sexual activity and sex play with other children, repeating what was done to him. He developed into a fairly large thirteen-year-old and was easily able to physically dominate and intimidate other children.

Mark also showed a chronic failure to learn in school, a consequence of many factors. One was his preoccupation with sexual matters which disrupted his ability to concentrate in school. Failure to learn is a common difficulty in children who have been sexually abused. Some of these children show an intellectual bewilderment, as if, having been overwhelmed by their emotions at a vulnerable time, they are now unable to understand and make sense out of the world around them. Mark's difficulties in trusting adults also meant that he could not accept help and knowledge from his teachers.

Mark's relationships with all adults, especially the child care staff, were highly ambivalent. With men, Mark was submissive, docile, and often fearful. He was afraid that a relationship with a man would expose him to sexual attack. Mark also admired men who were strong, and he wanted to build up his body and muscles in order to be able to defend himself.

With female staff, Mark alternated between being loud, defiant, and hostile, and being affectionate, coy, and babyish. This alteration is also typical of sexually abused and emotionally deprived children. On the one hand, Mark wanted to be the child who is loved, cared for, and protected, and he inappropriately (for a thirteen-year-old boy) expressed this by hanging onto and caressing female staff. On the other hand, Mark was angry at women, for he saw them as depriving—as his mother was. At times, he acted out that anger on female staff by being quarrelsome, verbally abusive, or even striking out. He repeated the pattern of conflict between the sexes that he was exposed to in his home environment.

Because of maternal rejection, deprivation, neglect, and the parental failure to protect him from environmental dangers, Mark showed intense anger toward his mother. In fantasy, children who have been either sexually or physically abused often direct considerable aggression toward their parents. In fantasy, the children may destroy the bad parents. In reality, they may show a paradoxically strong desire to be reunited with their parents, and direct their aggression against the substitute caretakers.

In Mark's fantasy, as revealed in psychological testing, his attitudes toward women were filled with violence and sadistic injury. He made up stories to pictures in which women, often identified as mothers, were repeatedly stabbed, shot, or strangled. In one story, the woman was dismembered by her killer, and in another, the body was mutilated. Strong sexual overtones ran through most of his stories. The stories clearly showed the fusion between sex and aggression, a legacy of Mark's environment.

Needless to say, Mark was extremely confused in his sexual identity. As a male, he had been the sexual object of another male. On the verge of adolescence, Mark found that his normal sexual object, the female, was someone with whom he was intensely angry. Mark's models for masculinity and femininity were poor ones, and his picture of the interaction between the sexes was even worse. Men dominate, fight with, and hurt women. Women deprive and reject men, and are victims of their brutality. Is it any wonder that Mark still has frequent nightmares of monsters and violence? Or that he did not respond to medication and continued to wet the bed three times a week?

Though Mark received some psychiatric help, he needed much more. He was discharged from the center to a residential treatment setting, where he is currently receiving intensive therapy.

While most people would not question that direct exposure to sexual activity with an adult affects a child, they overlook the impact of other forms of environmental sexual stimulation on the child. For example, a child may be more overstimulated by witnessing sexual behavior in the home than by being the object of sexual abuse. In the following case, a male child witnessed the unreported sexual abuse of a sibling, and the event caused disturbances in his behavior over the next few years.

Harry

Harry was admitted into a child care center when he was five years of age. He and his siblings had all been battered by their mother. The child caused no particular trouble in care, but there were indications from the child care workers that Harry was engaging in frequent masturbation and some sex play with other children.

A few months after his admission, Harry had a routine psychiatric evaluation. He undressed a number of dolls, noting their underpants carefully, removed these, and inspected the doll's crotch. He commented that boys are different from girls, but did not display any anxiety. The psychiatrist felt he showed a normal anatomical curiosity for his age.

At the end of his first year in care, the center's kindergarten teacher made the cryptic remark that "Harry has a rather sophisticated concept of sexual relationships." No more was said about this. Almost a year passed and Harry's living unit began to report more frequent escapades of sexual involvement with other children, frequent bed wetting, and occasional episodes of arson. It was decided to have Harry seen in individual therapy.

Harry was assigned a young, inexperienced, female social work student as a therapist. In the second session, he grabbed at the therapist's crotch and asked if that was where babies came from. She asked him not to grab her like that, answered his question, and was met by a demand to see her genitals. When she refused, Harry made an obscene gesture and told the therapist in explicit sexual language what she could do. The session ended on this note, leaving the young therapist feeling uncomfortable.

The next six months of therapy passed quietly with no reoccurrence of sexual material. Harry, however, was acting out sexually more and more in the living unit. Then, shortly after the therapist announced that she was leaving, the therapist and the seven-year-old boy had another disturbing session.

Harry pulled a toy gun on the therapist and ordered her to lie down on the floor. Had she been more experienced, she might have been more wary. As it was, she complied with the request. Harry promptly dropped the gun, jumped on top of the therapist, and made active sexual motions. When the surprised therapist pushed him off and jumped to her feet, Harry exposed himself. What followed next shattered the therapist's innocence. Harry said, "Let me hump you, please. Let me suck your tit. I won't tell anyone. It'll be our secret."

When the therapist told him no, Harry threw a temper tantrum, smashing toys and throwing the pieces at her. The therapist was unable to calm Harry down, and he left the session extremely angry at her.

In the next session, Harry spent all his time playing with cars and trucks, smashing them into each other and having accidents. He had the therapist make a sign that said: "Stop! Emergency! Do Not Get Close." Harry filled the air with sounds of sirens as police, fire trucks, and ambulances rushed to the scenes of the accidents.

In the last session, Harry showed considerable anger. The therapist made a standard interpretation, thinking Harry was angry because she was leaving. Harry immediately screamed back at her, "You're wrong. I'm angry because you won't let me hump you."

Therapy ended and over the summer Harry's sexual acting out continued. With the start of school in the fall, Harry was referred by the center's psychiatrist for a psychiatric reevaluation. In that session, he picked up a toy phone and called the police to hurry right over. The therapist, pretending he was the policeman, showed concern and asked: "What's wrong?"

Harry's reply was, "A big man hurt a little girl by jumping on her. The girl is crying because the man is hurting her." The "police" had to come and arrest the man and put him in jail. The "girl" went to the hospital in an ambulance.

Harry became very agitated and picked up a toy hammer and began to hit himself on the head. The therapist immediately stopped him, saying, "Why are you doing that? You are not a bad boy."

"I am a bad boy," Harry cried, and resumed hitting himself.

The therapist stopped him again and repeated, "Don't hurt yourself. You are a good boy." Having read the summary of the previous therapist's contacts with Harry, he continued, "You saw a man jump on a girl and hurt her. You jumped on your therapist like he did. Now you're worried that maybe you hurt her and you'll be sent away like the man was. You did not hurt her and you are not bad.

Nobody will send you away. Why don't you tell me about the man and the girl?"

Harry poured forth a story of seeing a man in his house sexually abuse one of his older sisters. It was not clear who the man was or which sister was involved, but Harry evidenced considerable anxiety and fear about the attack. Harry and his therapist discussed the matter in considerable detail, and Harry was relieved and reassured.

Remarkable changes in Harry's behavior followed this single session. The sexual acting out in the living unit stopped. Even more gratifying, Harry suddenly began learning in school. It was as if energy that had gone into trying to understand the sexual trauma had now been diverted into constructive learning in school.

Some months later, Harry dictated a story on a tape recorder in the center's school. In his story, Harry told about an eight-year-old boy who falls in love with his attractive teacher. The boy decides he is going to marry the teacher, but will wait until he is grown up. When he does grow up, they have a beautiful wedding. Afterwards Harry takes his bride to their new house. They enter the house and immediately go upstairs to the bedroom. Harry concluded his tape with the triumphant statement "And then did he ever hump her!"

At least Harry is placing things in some perspective. In his story, Harry sets aside sexual behavior for when he is grown up. For the time being, he is willing to return to the world of childhood and more appropriate concerns.

Commentary Harry had been traumatized by witnessing a sexual assault on his sister. In his immaturity, he did not understand what was happening. He did, however, sense the violent and aggressive nature of the act. That may have been more upsetting to him than the sexual aspects. Like many children, Harry tried to deal with the anxiety and fear this aroused in him by recreating the upsetting scene he had witnessed. In his recreation, Harry was no longer the helpless, frightened observer. Like Mark, he, too, now identified with the aggressor. With his female therapist, Harry probably repeated the same words he had heard the man say to his sister. A more experienced therapist might have picked up on the language and helped Harry to talk more about what was bothering him. The expression "It'll be our secret" should have been a clue.

Unfortunately, the young therapist reacted to the event as if it

were a sexual attack, attributing sexual motives to the child. So many
adults make this simple mistake of seeing the child's behavior as stem-
ming from the same sexual needs as adults. If one is to understand the
child's behavior, one must focus on the nonsexual feelings. It was when
the second therapist paid attention to the anxiety and guilt that Harry
shared with him the traumatic sexual event he had witnessed.

It is important to note that Harry's story came out after many
months of disturbed behavior and then only when a concerned mental
health professional helped Harry express the feelings that were trou-
bling him. Mark, on the other hand, avoided efforts to help him talk
about his relationship with his uncle. For both Mark and Harry, separating them from the adult sexual aggressor, while desirable, in no way
solved their problems. Both boys showed a preoccupation with sexual
matters and overt sexual behavior. For both boys, this behavior was a
symptom. Behind the sexual behavior were nonsexual feelings—fear,
guilt, and anxiety—that were upsetting them.

Dealing with the child victims of sexual abuse or overstimulation is
far from simple. Separating the child from the adult offender is sometimes a necessary first step, but the child needs far more than just a
change of environment. The disturbed sexual behavior of the child
is but the tip of an iceberg. Beneath the surface there are many other
related difficulties. One must look at the sexual abuse not as an isolated
episode, but rather in the context of the child's total emotional functioning. There will certainly be difficulties in emotional relationships
with others. Frequently there will be learning difficulties in school and
disturbed behavior in other areas. There will be feelings of guilt and
fear concerning sexual behavior.

Since the child victim was likely to have lived in an emotionally
deprived environment, the sexual relationship satisfied the child's need
for affection and closeness. Consequently, the child does not see the
adult's sexual attentions as being abusive. When separated from the
adult offender, the child often experiences a sense of loss, having been
deprived of an emotionally meaningful relationship. The child needs
help in handling his feelings of guilt and depression and needs to understand that the adult offender had problems and was unable to care for
him in an appropriate manner.

These two cases show how sexual difficulties are part of a
larger disturbed environment. If intervention is to help the child,

it must address itself to this environment that allows the abuse to occur.

The most healing experience for sexually abused children is to learn that there are adults who will care for them, protect them, and love them without overstimulating or overwhelming them with feelings of guilt and fear.

Chapter XVII
The Case of a Young Girl

The diagnosis of a disturbed sexual environment is a difficult one to make. In the absence of concrete signs, how does one know sexual abuse is occurring? One way is through direct revelation by either the child or his caretaker. Usually such knowledge is shared with an outsider only after a relationship of trust has been established with the child or caretaker. There is the possibility, especially with adolescent girls, that such revelations may be fantasy, but one should not be too quick to write off as fantasy what may be fact. The teen-age victim is often the last to be believed.

In the absence of direct revelation, a disturbed environment is diagnosed from observations of the child's behavior and/or from the parent-child interaction, supported by inferences from case history material. The following case will clarify the process of diagnosis of a disturbed sexual environment as well as illustrate the difficulties in interpersonal relationships that the environment created for the child.[1] The sexual behavior in this case was not traumatic for the child, but did affect her ways of seeking love and affection from adults.

Sally

Sally was admitted to a pediatric hospital as a potentially battered child after her mother told the emergency room staff, "I have just beaten her, and I'm afraid I'll kill her." On subsequent examinations, no bruises or evidence of trauma were noted. A skeletal survey for fractures was negative. Mother insisted that she had beaten the child a number of times in the past to the point of unconsciousness. She claimed the child never did anything right, and that she had to beat her to get her to do anything. "That kid is driving me crazy," mother told the staff, "I don't want to kill her and go to jail."

In the next few days, mother's concerns abruptly shifted from physical abuse to Sally's sexual behavior. "She is a fast woman," mother confided to a nurse. "She kisses like she means business, with her tongue out." Mother told of finding Sally naked in a closet with a boy on one occasion and of catching her masturbating with her doll on another.

Sally was *not* a teen-ager. At the time of her admission, the child was four and a half years old! Mother had long seen Sally as acting like a grown woman, especially in sexual areas. As a baby, she always "stared at you like an adult." As a newborn, Sally had breast and vaginal discharges, which her mother saw as signs of mature sexual functioning. This did not seem strange to the mother, who reported that she herself had menstruated at five years of age and was fully developed at nine.

In the hospital, Sally was insecure and frightened. She reacted negatively when she did not receive total attention. The slightest frustration would trigger a barrage of vulgar language. Sally spoke explicitly of sexual matters to the staff and acted out sexually with other children. During bath times, Sally would compulsively wash her genitals. She asked the nurse to touch her genitals because "I like you. My mommy does it to me, and she likes me." This incident led hospital staff to suspect that Sally had been sexually stimulated by her mother at home.

Sally was seen by a child psychiatrist who observed that her doll play was reflective of exposure to overt sexuality. She placed two dolls in a bed together and banged them violently against each other, while talking explicitly about sexual behavior. The mother denied that the child had witnessed her in sexual intercourse at home, but thought that Sally might have seen a baby sitter "doing it."

Because Sally was deemed to be a child in crisis (her hospital diagnosis was severe psychological disorder of early childhood), she was removed from the mother through court action and placed in foster care. The major reason for placement was the mother-child relationship—which the hospital staff saw as very negative—and the concerns about both physical and sexual abuse.

In foster care, there was no mention of any sexual difficulties or acting out. Instead, removed from the overstimulating home environment, Sally became quite aggressive and rough with other children. In this behavior she was partly repeating her physically abusive treatment at the hands of her mother. Sally was seen in individual therapy twice a week for many months.

Commentary   There are many factors in this case typical of battered child cases. The mother is a lonely woman. Without a husband and living in poverty, she cannot meet the needs of a child nor stand the normal demands that children place on adults. She was herself a battered child. She was beaten more than any of her sibs, but the more her parents battered her, the more she defied them. To make matters worse, Sally was the product of an unwanted pregnancy.

Observation of the mother-child interaction in the hospital showed the mother to be extremely rejecting of Sally, calling her "worthless and horrible." On one occasion, mother pushed the child away forcibly sending Sally crashing into a wall. The possibility that Sally has been and will continue to be physically abused by the mother must be taken seriously.

In looking over the case records of a number of foster children known to have been sexually abused, one is struck by the degree of violence present in these families. Many sexually abused children, like Sally, were also battered children. Others had parents whose main method of discipline was a blow. The children witnessed physical fights between the parents and were exposed to other acts of violence, such as knifings. In one case, a child witnessed the murder of a grandparent.

It seems likely that the environment exposed these children to premature and excessive stimulation of *both* sexual and aggressive feelings. Such stimulation overwhelms children, and they do not learn healthy means of control over these feelings. It is not surprising that the children perceived sexual behavior in violent terms, that is, someone being beaten and hurt. They may become adults for whom fighting is a way of making love. For others, violence brings sexual pleasure, a sadistic enjoyment in hurting others. Some, like Sally, will alternate between sexual and aggressive ways of relating to people.

In contacts with hospital staff, Sally's mother downplayed the physical abuse and turned her complaints solely to Sally's sexual behavior. Her complaints were a mixture of the commonplace—for example, masturbation—and the bizarre—the meaning she gave the breast and vaginal discharges. As such, the complaints point out one of the difficulties in working with young children, especially in the area of emotional and behavioral problems. What is reported as the child's problem is really the *adult's* perception. Much of the time parents are fairly accurate observers and reporters, but sometimes their interpretations are markedly at odds with "reality." Such was the case with Sally's mother, who saw the child as functioning as a sexually mature woman.

One might suspect that Sally's mother is seriously disturbed. A social worker who saw her felt she was a disorganized woman who at times appeared psychotic. She was evaluated by a psychiatrist who said that she was extremely "needy and primitive, but not psychotic." The mother's needs for love were so great that she used Sally to meet them. The mother-child relationship satisfied the mother's own momentary needs—she did not even see Sally's needs. The mother's primitiveness was reflected in the fact that she did not see Sally as a separate individual, but rather as an extension of herself. She even named the child after her. Her primitiveness was also shown by her impulsiveness and immature thinking patterns, such as projecting her own felt badness onto Sally.

In the hospital, direct observations of Sally's behavior showed a preoccupation with sexual matters. This suggested an overstimulating home environment. Direct sexual talk and open sexual behavior in front of adults is rare in children. These behaviors do occur, but usually out of sight of adults. When such behavior is open, it indicates that the child has sexual concerns that are troublesome. The child brings them out into the open in the hope that the adult will recognize them and help him or her deal with them. Often the child is looking for information and reassurance that the behavior is acceptable, or relief from guilty and anxious feelings.

In other children, direct indications of a disturbed sexual environment might be excessive masturbation or exposure of the genitals. On a more indirect level, nightmares can be an indication of sexual overstimulation and anxiety, as can bed wetting and/or pyromania. These symptoms can also be related to aggressive concerns. At a more general level, the fear of a physical examination, or specifically a genital exam, may suggest an underlying sexual anxiety. The fear of a caretaking adult of the opposite sex may have a sexual basis. Certain age inappropriate behaviors, such as excessive clinging to the adult, seductive behavior, or blatant rubbing up against the adult, may be other clues of an overstimulating environment. Children who are overstimulated by strong feelings usually translate them into some form of motor activity.

The presence of either blatant or subtle clues may suggest a further look into the child's background for signs of a deviant sexual environment. In Sally's case, the overstimulation of sexual feelings can probably be traced directly to mother's manipulation of Sally's genitals during bath times. In some cases there may be other forms of direct sexual stimulation. In still other cases the environmental overstimulation may be indirect. For example, children can be sexually stimulated by crowded sleeping conditions, where the child shares a bed with a sibling or a parent of the opposite sex; the lack of privacy and modesty in the family; having parents walk around the house in the nude; having a pregnant mother; witnessing adult sexual activity; taking a shower with an adult; or even receiving inappropriate sex education information. Of course, it is not just the simple presence of any of these behaviors that is crucial, but rather how they fit into the child's total environment, including factors such as the child's age, vulnerability, and past experiences.

From the case record, it was possible to pick up early clues that the mother-child relationship in Sally's case was to be a troubled one. The prenatal nurse was in an excellent position to have seen the difficulties shaping up in regard to this pregnancy. It wasn't until the beginning of the fifth month of the pregnancy that Sally's mother sought out prenatal care. Though vitamins and iron were prescribed by a physician, she did not take them. The medical history taken at this time revealed that there had been two prior miscarriages. The mother informed the nurse that this was an unwanted pregnancy, and that her husband had deserted her when he found out about it. As the pregnancy drew to a close, the mother had to give up a job that she enjoyed in order to have Sally. She voiced her resentment about this to a nurse. While none of these clues are decisive in themselves, they do add up to a pattern of a mother who experienced considerable conflict over her pregnancy. These attitudes can be the foundation of a rejecting, neglecting, or physically abusive mother.

To the postnatal nurse, there were also signs of trouble in the mother-child interaction. The description of the child "staring at me like an adult" is one. When a mother complains of unusual hostility on the child's part toward her, this is usually an indication that mother herself has strong negative feelings toward the child. Another clue was the "breast and vaginal discharges." The meaning of these to mother is indicative of her own disturbed sexuality and can only bode ill for the mother-child relationship.

There was further evidence in the history that the relationship was not going well. At six weeks, Sally was hospitalized with diaper rash and diarrhea. The admission was noteworthy in that Sally had become ill while being cared for by another woman. Mother had abruptly turned the care of Sally over to a friend for an indefinite period of time because she was "tired of caring for her." When an infant is abandoned for indefinite periods for ill-defined reasons, the mother is expressing negative feelings about her role as a mother and her relationship to the child.

When Sally was hospitalized as a potentially battered child, there was yet another opportunity for a professional to help Sally. During the bathing incident, Sally asked the nurse to touch her genitals. To an adult not secure in her own sexuality, Sally's request was a threatening invitation. The temptation is to be punitive and rejecting of Sally. Again, the inclination is for the nurse to place an adult interpretation on Sally's behavior, to see this as a sexual invitation and to react accordingly.

One needs to look at this interaction through the child's eyes. It is a perfect example of a child who is seeking affection from an adult in the context of a sexual relationship. Sally sees the nurse as an extension of her mother. She expects this adult to react to her in the only way Sally knows adults can act, as her mother does. Hence, Sally expects the nurse to be inconsistent, that is, to alternate between hostility, rejection, and physical abuse on the one hand, and seductive and sexually overstimulating behavior on the other. Mother shows her love for Sally by overstimulating her sexually. To Sally, this means being *loved,* not abused.

The role of the nurse is to help Sally make a transition in her relationships with adults. Sally has come to see the nurse as a different person from mother. In a sense, Sally is testing the adults in her new environment of the hospital to see if they are like her mother.

This period of testing by the child is very difficult for the adults who try to care for Sally. They need to be patient and consistent. Sally's behavior can arouse complex feelings in adults, for example, anger, disgust, anxiety, or shock. Acting on any of these feelings would not be helpful to Sally.

The nurse declined Sally's invitation to touch her genitals, while reassuring her that she did like her, pointing out things she did that showed she liked Sally—bathing her, feeding her, giving her a hug and a kiss, talking to her, and so forth. Sally does not need moral lectures on sex, nor to hear negative opinions about mothers who sexually stimulate their children.

In foster care, the adults who care for Sally will also be tested. They must be careful not to make adult value judgments about what the child does or says. For Sally to unlearn patterns of relating to adults that she has learned from her mother, she must first come to realize that there are alternate ways of relating that are satisfying. Adults can show Sally ways of relating that are different from her mother's. They do this not by taking on artificial roles, but by being themselves. A caring adult's most valuable resource for treatment is his or her own personality.

"I don't have to touch you there to show I like you" can be a therapeutic response. Touching Sally's genitals would be acting like her mother. It would also be overstimulating to Sally. Prolonged physical contact will also overstimulate her. A hug and a kiss are appropriate—they do not involve a protracted period of caressing and fondling.

Often adults are hesitant to make a response until they are sure how much the child understands about sex. The important issue is not what the child understands about sex, but rather what the adult understands about the child's needs. Sally needs to be shown loving acceptance in a way that doesn't overstimulate her. A child can be traumatized by the arousal of strong feelings with which she or he is emotionally too immature to deal. It does not matter what the feeling is. It may be anxiety, grief, abandonment, excitement, panic, or anger. A child who is flooded with stimulation uses all his or her energy to ward off the feeling of being overwhelmed and threatened with destruction of his personality. She or he has no resources left to learn how to master the feeling.

One of the ways a child wards off overstimulation is by recreating the very situation which first aroused the feeling. It is as if the child believes that by creating the situation, she or he can control it when the feeling appears. The self-induced exposure is repeated with the hope that successive experiences will weaken the intensity of the feeling, that is, it won't be so frightening or painful the sixth time around.

Thus, many children are driven to repeat their past to recreate the very situation that scares them. Sally invites the sexual advance, but part of her hopes it won't happen this time. The other part of her wants what the experience means, that she is loved by her mother. A caretaking adult must give Sally the love she wants without the overstimulation she fears. When Sally's needs for love are met in other ways, she will no longer have to initiate the sexual behavior that brought her mother's love. She will then concentrate solely on expressing the other strong feeling that overwhelms her: anger at mother for rejecting and battering her.

The sexual environment in this case determined how Sally attempted to get love from people. It should not blind us to other aspects of her childhood environment, namely, that underneath the blatant sexual behavior there is an angry, frightened, and unhappy child. This was clear when Sally was removed from the disturbed sexual home environment and placed in foster care. Her sexual behavior was replaced by aggressive behavior toward other children. It is anger at being rejected that is the major stumbling block to Sally's healthy growth and development. It is anger that will be the core of the psychotherapeutic work with Sally, not sex.

Sally was the product of learned experiences with her mother, who was Sally's first and virtually only teacher. Sally carries these learned expectations of how adults will act into her other relationships. Sally's mother was not able to help her grow up, but the mother's limitations are not necessarily Sally's. Sally can still be helped by caring adults who set different examples for her. Over time, these caretaking adults can show Sally better images of what it is to be an adult.

CONCLUSION
An End to Sexual Abuse?

Society is very reluctant to face this ugly aspect of our civilization [child sex abuse]. The harsh reality is, that despite our vaunted progress and accomplishments, we are still unable to protect the most vulnerable members of our society from the cruelties of others. This failure is so difficult to face that it usually elicits denial.[1]

It does not take a perceptive person to realize that sexual abuse of children is difficult to prevent mainly because the very people one relies upon to protect children betray them. About three fourths of the sexual offenses against children are committed by adults whom the child knows and trusts.

What can be done to put an end to the sexual abuse of children? Is it possible to prevent child sex abuse? Following are steps that could be taken to deal effectively with the problem:

1. One concrete manifestation of the fact that we fail to protect our children is that we have no national reporting system for cases of child sexual abuse, hence, our knowledge of the extent of the problem is limited. Uniform state laws are needed that define sexual abuse in detail, and penalties and treatment of offenders need to to be standardized. There is also a need for national forms for the reporting of child sexual abuse. In addition, each state should establish a single tollfree hot line for that state to facilitate the reporting of suspected child abuse and sexual abuse cases to the appropriate authorities. (Early in 1979, Massachusetts will be getting a hot line, and it is expected that this will increase the number of cases of child abuse reported from the present 1400 a month to about 2200 a month.)[2]

2. There is a need for a broad public educational program on child

sexual abuse. Public awareness and discussion of the problem must be promoted, beginning with the education of the public on the use of a hot line and the need to report cases of child sexual abuse. The largest single obstacle to doing something about child sexual abuse is the public's attitude of secrecy. It prevents victims and families from seeking and obtaining help. Child sexual abuse will not magically disappear if we do not talk about it. Rather, child sexual abuse thrives on secrecy.

A public educational program should also include information about the nature and incidence of child sexual abuse, and the community resources available to help children, parents, and offenders. As part of the program, specific information about the needs of children and how to parent adequately should be made available. Courses in parenting and child care should be an essential part of the public school curriculum.

3. Child sexual abuse cases often come from families in which one or both parents have a history of sexual abuse as children. One of the effects of sexual abuse is that the child victim grows into an adult who is more likely to sexually abuse his or her own children. Thus, an absolutely essential step in any program of prevention is to guarantee psychiatric treatment to all identified child victims of sexual abuse. Communities need to institute treatment programs specifically geared to treating the families and victims of sexual abuse.

4. Many experts agree that the real trauma of child sexual abuse begins when it is discovered. This remark usually refers to the insensitive handling of the victim—and family—by the social and legal systems. Some people go so far as to claim that the child's contact with the police, courts, and lawyers is often more traumatic than the original sexual assault, and advise against exposing the child to this process. Inhumane and traumatic handling of child sexual abuse cases is not limited to judges, lawyers, police, and probation officers, however. It is also widespread among physicians and hospital personnel, social workers, child care workers, schoolteachers, and even psychiatric personnel in child guidance clinics.

In order to help the child victim, all agencies and individuals dealing with child sexual abuse cases must coordinate their efforts. Professionals must be trained and educated to deal with cases of child sexual abuse. The people involved must come to understand the needs of the victims, family, and offender. They must be helped so that their own feelings don't get in the way of rational, helpful action. Let me cite an example of the handling of a child victim to illustrate what I mean.[3]

A six-year-old girl was brought to a hospital because her mother discovered blood in the child's panties that morning. For the next few hours in the hospital, the child was badgered by her father, a nurse, and two doctors, all trying to get the frightened child to tell them what had happened to her.

A more sensitive doctor saw the child alone for forty-five minutes, played games with her, and role-played what had happened. He found out that the girl's older sister's boyfriend had molested the child.

When the father was told, he denied that such a thing was possible. He was sure the child had been abused by an elderly man in the neighborhood who often gave the children candy and invited them into his apartment. He tried to get the child to admit that this was what had really happened. He scolded her for disobedience when she denied it.

Then the physicians moved in for a genital examination, and took blood samples and anal and vaginal cultures. The screaming child had to be held down by two nurses during these procedures. When it was over, she was left lying naked on a hospital stretcher. The father came back into the room to stay with her, renewed his questioning, and became increasingly angry with the child's answers. At this point, the police arrived. A burly policeman approached the crying, unclothed child on the stretcher and growled, "Has someone been messing with you?" The child refused to answer, thereby demonstrating that she was virtually the only one in the situation with any good sense.

Now contrast this horror story with one of a police officer who either had a good deal of common sense or had had some professional training in dealing with children.

A five-year-old boy arrived home stark naked and clutching a bag of candy. His parents took one look at him and promptly went into hysterics. They so frightened the child that he refused to speak. The police were called.

The police officer chatted with the boy for a while to put him at ease. He commented on the bag of candy. The child shyly offered him some, but the officer refused.

"I don't want to take yours," he told the boy, "but I'd like a bag of my own." He then suggested that the boy might like to ride around with him in the police car and see if they could find the man who was giving away the free candy. The child agreed and led the officer to the area where the assault occurred.

There are many helpful materials available to professionals who would like to improve their ability to handle child sexual abuse cases. Burgess and Holmstrom discuss interviewing of young rape victims in their book. The Queen's Bench Foundation in San Francisco puts out guidelines for the medical management of sexually abused children. Their material includes the physician's sexual assault checklist from the San Francisco General Hospital. Also included are helpful booklets for parents printed in English, Spanish, and Chinese, discussing the sexual abuse of children.[4] Sgroi has discussed the medical management of child sexual assault cases.[5] Other organizations put out primers for parents, guidelines for professionals, and special techniques for child witnesses.[6] This material needs to be organized and distributed to specific target groups of professionals and parents.

5. Professionals as well as the public need help with their feelings about child sexual abuse. The usual reaction in most people is an emotional and punitive one. In such a climate it is difficult to find much support for preventive, treatment, and rehabilitation programs. The public needs to understand that the incarceration of an offender does not solve the problem unless one intends to keep all sex offenders locked up until the day they die. In the case of incest, removing the father from the home may destroy the family. Placing the child in foster care may destroy the child. Nor does divorce solve the problem, for some offenders remarry and abuse the children of their new family.

6. In a broader sense, prevention of sexual abuse of children is part of a larger need for developing healthier attitudes toward sex. Perhaps only a limited amount of change through education is possible with those individuals who are already adults. However, much can be done with the coming generation through a universal, no-nonsense sex education program in the public schools, starting with kindergarten children. Of course, information on the sexual abuse of children would be a part of the curriculum. Some experts have suggested that the most important thing in preventing sexual abuse is teaching children they have a right to say "no." Obviously one cannot rely upon certain parents to teach their children this.

Women Organized Against Rape (WOAR) in Philadelphia puts out a pamphlet entitled, "Discussing Rape with Children." This advice is given to children:

No one has the right to touch any part of your body without your consent. No one has the right to touch your bottom or your pants, except your parents, the doctor, or the nurse. They should always have your consent.[7]

This is certainly a step in the right direction. The "except" is troublesome. Perhaps it should be "even." I doubt that children will understand this concept of consent. I am not convinced that a child saying "no" would be sufficient to stop an incestual attack. After all, the person he or she says "no" to is one whom the child is also taught she or he must obey. Children might be better off instructed that if someone touches them or does something to make them uncomfortable, they should report it to another adult they trust, such as a parent, a teacher, or a neighbor. I taught one adolescent incest victim with whom I worked to say "no" by screaming her head off if her father tried to touch her. Her screams alerted her mother, who was then able to protect the child.

7. Rosenfeld, in an article in the *Journal of the American Medical Association,* believes there is a pressing need for research into the sexual misuse of children.[8] Federal funds from the National Center on Child Abuse and Neglect are needed for research into family functioning in abusive situations and the factors that lead to sexual abuse. Such information is essential for both prevention and treatment.

8. We know that physical and sexual abuse often take place because of dysfunctions in family life. Some of the danger signs in families are known and include social isolation of the child and family; unavailable mother or father; a parental history of abuse; poor spouse relationships; a father with poor impulse control and possibly an alcohol or drug abuse problem; emotional deprivation of children, which leads them to search for human contact in inappropriate ways; the daughter who takes over mother's role in the family; parents who do not protect their child; poverty; and loss of job. Thus part of preventing sexual abuse of children must necessarily involve general programs to strengthen families. Obvious examples are day care centers, homemaker services, family counseling services, and parent education courses.

9. The handling of sexual abuse cases and the relevant laws should be rethought. Instead of the legal response being based upon our emotional horror at the crime, the more serious crimes should be those which involve force or violence, those which are repetitive in nature, or those which contain an exploitative profit element (for

example, the pimp should be dealt with more severely than the prostitute).

Rowland reports that some European countries have substituted a system whereby a panel of psychologists screen each child sexual abuse case.[9] If the child has suffered no apparent ill effects, the case is declared to be of no importance and is handled outside of the court system. Essentially "victimless" crimes should not be considered crimes.

10. Crimes of violence involving young people are on the increase. Nearly half of all those arrested for violent crimes are teen-agers (average age, fifteen years). Seventy-five percent of all violent street crimes are committed by persons twenty-five years of age or younger, and this same age group accounts for 44 percent of all murders.[10] A million children, most of them teen-agers, run away from their homes each year, many ending up as prostitutes.

Perhaps this country could form a teen-age domestic Peace Corps that would draft all teen-agers not in school (or all children when they reach sixteen years of age) into one to two years of paid service to their country. The corps would work in social welfare areas—hospital aides, recreational workers, neighborhood clean-up crews, forestry projects—and could perhaps be located near participants' homes. If we can draft teen-agers to defend their country, why not draft them to improve it? To avoid "involuntary servitude," they would be paid minimum wage.

The value of such a program would be to give teen-agers a social purpose, to help them earn money, to encourage them to contribute to their society, to help them develop a social consciousness, and to provide supervision. The program could tie in with job training and experience, and could give them exposure to different jobs and the opportunity to learn vocational skills. The program might also involve some humanistic education. Such a program would have to be developed and led by sensitive and caring people. It could not be run like a school, a prison, or a paramilitary organization.

A Further Suggestion

I would like to suggest one further, frankly utopian, idea. Throughout this book I have pointed out many dilemmas and problems that plague our society. As a society, we recently achieved our two-hundredth birthday marking the signing of the Declaration of Independence. In a few years (1987) we will mark the two-hundredth anniversary of the signing of the Constitution, the legal document upon which our society is founded.

I can think of no better way to celebrate these events than to establish a Quality of Life Council. This group would attempt to assess and evaluate the quality of life in our country, pointing out the strengths and weaknesses.

The council would be an on-going body. Its role would be to help set national priorities for the improvement of the quality of life for all citizens. It would help focus national attention on social concerns. It would serve as an overall guiding force, to advise and recommend to the federal and state governments those areas of social policy and programs in need of attention. The council could integrate and coordinate programs and policies so that we would have a consistent and rational approach to social problems rather than the random, often conflicting, proliferation of programs and policies that we have now.

The council might also involve and educate the public through discussions of social policy. The council would also develop innovative "solutions" to national social problems. The council would function as an advocate for special groups, such as children. Much like the economic advisers, military advisers, and others who advise the government now, the Quality of Life Council would have consistent input on social policy. It would consider our society as a single, dynamic entity.

Many of our problems today arise out of conflicts of competing social policies. Throughout this book I have indicated many such conflicts that need resolution. Examples are the rights of children versus the rights of parents—adoption and termination of parental rights in foster care are but two examples; the role of television in our society; developing sensible guidelines for a sane sexual life for adolescents; the role of violence in our society; corporal punishment in children's institutions; the role of pornography and obscenity in our society; discrepancies in state laws in the treatment of children; the rights of individuals versus the protection of society; the handling of victimless crimes; the conflict between promoting children's rights and protecting their welfare; the extent to which the state can force treatment on an involuntarily committed offender versus the public's right to protection from certain types of crimes. These are just a few of the areas that a Quality of Life Council might consider. One can easily think of many other conflicts and discrepancies between social policy and social programs that might be addressed.

 The greatest area that needs attention and consideration is the quality of life for children in America. Sexual abuse, which has been the concern of this book, is only one aspect of this more general problem.

During the final week of writing this book, I found the following stories in the local newspaper:

A Massachusetts police officer is indicted on thirteen counts of unnatural acts and rape of a child.

A thirty-year-old woman tells a meeting of the American Nurses Association of her sexual relations with her father and how it left permanent scars on her self-esteem and normal social development. "For more than fifteen years I was fooled into believing I was a willing party, and that it was my fault that all this happened."

An eleven-year-old girl is brutally beaten and tortured, and dies from her injuries. Her father and stepmother are indicted on charges of first degree murder. The district attorney claims the child has been sexually abused as well.[11]

The sad and tragic toll of wasted children's lives goes on each day. It is going on even now.

Notes

INTRODUCTION: THE LAST FRONTIER

1. C. Henry Kempe et al., "The Battered-Child Syndrome," *Journal of the American Medical Association,* Vol. 181 (1962): 17.

2. *American Orthopsychiatric Association Newsletter* (Summer 1976): 8.

3. "The Battered Children," *Newsweek,* 10 October 1977, 112B.

4. *AOA Newsletter,* p. 8.

5. See note 3.

6. David R. Walters, *Physical and Sexual Abuse of Children* (Bloomington, Indiana: Indiana University Press, 1975), p. 29.

7. Renee S. T. Brant and Veronica Tisza, "The Sexually Misused Child," *American Journal of Orthopsychiatry* (January 1977): 81.

8. E. Weber, "Sexual Abuse Begins at Home," *Ms.* (April 1977): 64.

9. A. Kinsey et al., *Sexual Behavior in the Human Female* (Philadelphia: W. B. Saunders, 1953), pp. 116–122. Kinsey described 52 percent of those 1075 contacts as exhibitionism; 31 percent as fondling; 27 percent as manipulation of the male or female genitalia; 2 percent as oral sex, and 3 percent as coitus.

10. *Philadelphia Evening Bulletin.* 11 November 1977, p. A21.

11. Ibid.

12. "Reporting Abuse and Neglect," *Children Today* (May/June 1977): 26.

13. Suzanne M. Sgroi, "Sexual Molestation of Children," *Children Today* (May/June 1975): 19–20, Table 2.

14. A. A. Rosenfeld et al., "The Sexual Misuse of Children—A Brief Survey," *Psychiatric Opinion* (April 1976): 8.

15. A. I. Hartley and R. Ginn, "Reporting Child Abuse," *Texas Medicine* (February 1975): 84.

CHAPTER I: WHAT IS RAPE?

1. A. Nicholas Groth and Ann W. Burgess, "Rape: A Sexual Deviation," *American Journal of Orthopsychiatry* (July 1977): 403–404.

2. Groth, "Sexual Dysfunction During Rape," *New England Journal of Medicine* (6 October 1977): 764.

3. "Some Violence Statistics," *American Psychological Association Monitor* (February 1978): 4.

4. M. J. Kirkpatrick, "Medical Resistance to Treating Rape Victims," *Psychiatric Opinion* (July/August 1977): 22. See also, "Rape—Myths and Realities," a 2-page mimeograph handout by WOAR (Women Organized Against Rape), 1220 Sansom Street, Philadelphia, PA 19107.

5. A. F. Schiff, "A Statistical Evaluation of Rape," *Forensic Science* 2 (1973): 339–349.

6. *Boston Globe*, 2 August 1978, p. 4.

7. *Boston Globe*, 6 June 1978, p. 20.

8. *Boston Globe*, 15 September 1978, p. 52.

9. *Boston Globe*, 10 February 1978, p. 28. See also "Briefs: Sex Education," *Time* (27 February 1978): 85.

CHAPTER II: CHILD RAPE—REALITIES AND MYTHS

1. S. J. Hursch, *The Trouble with Rape* (Chicago: Nelson-Hall, 1977), p. 8.

2. B. Herjanic and R. P. Wilbois, "Sexual Abuse of Children," *Journal of the American Medical Association* (23 January 1978): 331.

3. *Boston Globe*, 26 December 1977, p. 19.

4. "Discussing Rape with Children," WOAR (Women Organized Against Rape) pamphlet, p. 11.

5. Hursch, p. 22.

6. Ann W. Burgess and Lynda L. Holmstrom, "Sexual Trauma of Children and Adolescents," *Nursing Clinics of North America* (September 1975): 552.

7. M. Solomon, "The Sexually Abused Child—Guidelines for Professionals," a mimeographed pamphlet by Metro's Rape Awareness Public Education Program, hereinafter referred to as Metro fact sheet, 140 West Flagler Street, Miami, FL 33130.

8. The Child Protection Unit Children's Hospital National Medical Center in Washington, D.C., reports: offender's home, 22 percent; child's home, 35 percent. Metro Rape Awareness (Miami, Florida) reports: for girls, two-thirds in home of victim or offender; for boys, one-half.

9. J. J. Peters, "Children Who Are Victims of Sexual Assault and the Psychology of Offenders," *American Journal of Psychotherapy* (July 1976): 416.

10. Peters, p. 415.

11. Peters, p. 416.

12. Women Organized Against Rape, data report, 21 December 1977, p. 3. The statistics are as follows: 73 percent one attacker; 13 percent by two attackers; 14 percent by more than two.

13. Peters, p. 416.

14. A. Nicholas Groth and H. J. Birnbaum, "Adult Sexual Orientation and Attraction to Underage Persons," *Archives of Sexual Behavior*, Vol. 7: 3 (1978), 179, and Table I, 178.

15. Suzanne M. Sgroi, "Sexual Molestation of Children," *Children Today* (May/June 1975): 18.

16. J. Voigt, "Sexual Offenses in Copenhagen: A Medicolegal Study," *Forensic Science* 1 (1972): 68, Table II.

17. D. R. Walters, *Physical and Sexual Abuse of Children* (Bloomington, Indiana: University of Indiana Press, 1975), pp. 111–133.

18. Hursch, p. 31.

19. WOAR pamphlets "Discussing Rape with Children," p. 11, and "Rape—Myths and Realities," p. 2.

20. Metro fact sheet, p. 2. J. J. Peters agrees and adds 66 percent are during daylight hours or at dusk, and that Monday and Friday are the most frequent days for an attack on a child (Peters, p. 415).

For all rapes—adult and child—WOAR reports that most rapes occur on Saturday; 57 percent are committed between 8 P.M. and 4 A.M.; 68 percent of all rapes were indoors; and 27 percent were in the victim's home.

In the Copenhagen study, Voigt reports on 650 adult and child sexual offenses, including rapes: 47 percent between 6 P.M. and 6 A.M.; 14 percent between 6 A.M. and noon; 39 percent between noon and 6 P.M. In addition, almost two thirds of sexual offenses were committed between April and September and one third from October to March.

21. Vincent De Francis, "Protecting the Child Victim of Sex Crimes Committed by Adults," *American Humane Association,* Denver, 1969.

22. A. A. Rosenfeld et al., "The Sexual Misuse of Children," *Psychiatric Opinion* (April 1976): 8.

23. J. Ensminger and S. A. Ferguson, *Sexual Assault of Children.* Paper presented at Fifth Biennial NASW Professional Symposium, San Diego, California, November 1977, p. 2.

24. L. G. Schultz, "The Child Sex Victim," *Child Welfare* (March 1973): 149, 155.

25. J. Gagnon and W. Simon, "The Child Molester—Surprising Advice For Worried Parents," *Redbook* (February 1969): 55.

26. A. Nicholas Groth and Ann W. Burgess, "Motivational Intent in the Sexual Assault of Children," *Criminal Justice and Behavior* (September 1977): 263.

27. M. J. Kirkpatrick, "Medical Resistance to Rape Victims," *Phychiatric Opinion* (July/August 1977): 19. In 75 to 93 percent of cases, the rapist used some degree of force; 21 to 33 percent of these cases involved weapons. WOAR data report, p. 3. Forty-three percent of adult victims are threatened by a weapon (knives 20 percent and guns 10 percent of total).

28. Groth and Birnbaum, p. 178, Table I, and p. 179. The high percentage of violence (20 percent) in this sample may seem to contradict the figure above, that only 5 percent of child sexual assaults involve forced penetration with violent attack on the child. The difference in Groth's sample is of *convicted* sex offenders at a treatment center for sexually dangerous persons, and hence one might expect a higher incidence of violent offenders.

29. Muriel Solomon, "Sex Abuse Guidelines for Teenagers," Metro Rape Awareness Public Education Program, p. 1.

30. Voigt, p. 73, and Table X, p. 75.

31. Herjanic and Wilbois, p. 331.

32. "Some Violence Statistics," *American Psychological Association Monitor* (February 1978): 4. R. DeVine says: one-third of all cases will not go to trial and 44 percent of cases taken to court will be dismissed because of lack of evidence ("Sexual Abuse—Who Cares?" in *Child Abuse Conference Proceedings,* Children's Hospital National Medical Center, February 1977, p. 81). In 1972, only 133 out of every 1000 men tried for rape were convicted, the lowest rate for any violent crime (Kirkpatrick, p. 20).

33. Voigt, p. 68, Table II, by extrapolation.

34. Groth and Birnbaum, pp. 177, 179, and Table I, p. 178 (extrapolated).

35. "Some Violence Statistics," *American Psychological Association Monitor* (February 1978): 4. Nearly 50 percent of all arrests for violent crimes are teenagers, and the age of the greatest number of arrests is fifteen. Of all violent street crimes, 75 percent are committed by persons twenty-five years of age or younger, including 44 percent of all murders.

CHAPTER III· TRAUMATIC EFFECTS OF RAPE

1. Ann W. Burgess and Lynda L. Holmstrom, *Rape! Victims of Crisis.* (R. J. Brady Co., 1974), especially pp. 37ff.

2. J. J. Peters, "Children Who Are Victims of Sexual Assault and the Psychology of Offenders," *American Journal of Psychotherapy* (July 1976): 414.

3. Burgess and Holmstrom, "Sexual Trauma of Children and Adolescents," *Nursing Clinics of North America* (September 1975): 551–563.

4. Burgess and Holmstrom, *Rape! Victims of Crisis,* p. 55 (Table I).

5. Peters, "Child Rape: Defusing a Psychological Time Bomb," *Hospital Physician* (February 1973): 46.

6. Amy Katan, "Children Who Were Raped," *Psychoanalytic Study of the Child,* vol. 28 (1973): 220.

CHAPTER IV: OFFENDERS AND TREATMENT

1. Remarks of Maddi-Jane Stern, M.S.W., A.C.S.W., Director Social Service, Center for Rape Concern, at WOAR conference on *The Many Faces of Rape,* Philadelphia, Pa., January 18–21, 1978.

2. A. N. Groth and H. J. Birnbaum, "Adult Sexual Orientation and Attraction to Underage Persons," *Archives of Sexual Behavior,* Vol. 7: 3 (1978): 175–181.

3. F. A. Henn et al., "Forensic Psychiatry: Profiles of Two Types of Sex Offenders," *American Journal of Psychiatry* (June 1976): 694.

4. J. J. Peters, "Children Who Are Victims of Sexual Assault and the Psychology of Offenders," *American Journal of Psychotherapy* (July 1976): 408–413.

5. *Boston Globe,* 2 March 1978, p. 25.

6. *Philadelphia Inquirer,* 18 December 1977, p. 1.

7. *New York Times,* 21 May 1974, p. 37.

CHAPTER V: THE NATURE OF THE PROBLEM

1. J. Herman and L. Hirschman, "Father-Daughter Incest," *Signs* (Summer 1977): 736.

2. G. Pauley, "Of Cries, Whispers and Incest," in *Philadelphia Evening Bulletin,* 3 October 1977, p. A8.

3. Herman and Hirschman, p. 736.

4. J. J. Young, "Incest," *Playgirl* (January 1978): 68.

5. H. Giarretto, "The Treatment of Father-Daughter Incest," *Children Today* (July/August 1976): 4.

6. E. Weber, "Sexual Abuse Begins at Home," *Ms.* (April 1977): 65.

7. R. Farson, *Birthrights* (New York: Macmillan, 1974), p. 148. Farson's source was J. Woodbury and E. Schwartz, *The Silent Sin* (New York: New American Library, 1971).

8. For example, in Santa Clara County, California, Giarretto found the 400 incest families referred to his program were representative of the racial composition of the county (76.8 percent white; 17.5 percent Mexican American; 3 percent Oriental; and 1.7 percent black). The make-up of the work force tended toward professional, semiprofessional, and skilled blue-collar groups. Average family income was $13,413 and median educational level was 12.6 years (Giarretto, p. 4).

9. Pauley, "Incest: Healing Taboo's Harsh Wounds," in *Philadelphia Evening Bulletin,* 4 October 1977, p. 22.

10. R. Green, "Victim of Child Abuse Tells Her Story," in *Boston Globe,* 9 September 1977, p. 12.

11. J. Petroccia, "Endwell Woman Provides Therapy for Victims of Society's Last Taboo," in *Birghamton* (New York) *Press and Sun Bulletin.* 19 February 1978, p. 3C.

12. "Of Cries, Whispers and Incest," p. 8.

13. Ibid.

14. Ann W. Burgess et al., *Sexual Assault of Children and Adolescents* (Lexington, Mass: Lexington Books, 1978), p. 21.

15. Robert Geiser and Sister M. Norberta, "Sexual Disturbance in Young Children," *Maternal Child Nursing* (May/June 1976): 188.

CHAPTER VI: FATHER-DAUGHTER INCEST

1. Hector Cavallin, "Incestuous Fathers: A Clinical Report," *American Journal of Psychiatry* (April 1966): 1132.

2. Amy Katan, "Children Who Were Raped," *Psychoanalytic Study of the Child,* Vol. 28 (1973): 219.

3. For an excellent article on the family dynamics of incest, see I. Kaufman et al., "The Family Constellation and Overt Incestuous Relations between Father and Daughter," *American Journal of Orthopsychiatry* 24 (1954): 266. See also N. Lustig et al., "Incest," *Archives of General Psychiatry* (January 1966): 31–39.

4. Remarks of Alexander G. Zaphiris, School of Social Work, University of Denver, at the National Conference on Child Abuse and Neglect, New York City, April 16–19, 1978.

5. Kaufman et al.

6. For a further discussion of foster care, see Robert Geiser, *The Illusion of Caring* (Boston: Beacon Press, 1973).

7. J. Herman and L. Hirschman, "Father-Daughter Incest," *Signs* (Summer 1977): 750.

8. Judianne Densen-Gerber and J. Benward, "Incest as a Causative Factor in Anti-Social Behavior," *Child Abuse Conference Proceedings,* Children's Hospital National Medical Center, February 1977, Washington, D.C., pp. 84–85.

9. E. Weber, "Sexual Abuse Begins at Home," *Ms.* (April 1977): 64.

10. Weber, p. 65.

11. Kaufman et al., p. 268.

12. L. Heims and I. Kaufman, "Variations on a Theme of Incest," *American Journal of Orthopsychiatry* 33 (1963): 312.

CHAPTER VII: THE TREATMENT OF FATHER-DAUGHTER INCEST

1. I have based my description of the CSATP primarily on H. Giarretto, "The Treatment of Father-Daughter Incest," *Children Today,* (July/August 1976): 2–5, 34–35; H. Giarretto, A. Giarretto, and S. Sgroi, "Coordinated Community Treatment of Incest," in Ann W. Burgess et al., *Sexual Assault of Children and Adolescents* (Lexington, Mass.: Lexington Books, 1978), pp. 231–240.

CHAPTER VIII: OTHER TYPES OF INCEST

1. W. H. Masters and V. E. Johnson, "Incest: The Ultimate Sexual Taboo," *Redbook* (April 1976): 54.

2. C. W. Wahl, "The Psychodynamics of Consummated Maternal Incest," *Archives of General Psychiatry* 3 (1960): 188.

3. G. A. Awad, "Father-Son Incest: A Case Report," *Journal of Nervous and Mental Disease* (February 1976): 135.

4. P. Rossman, *Sexual Experience between Men and Boys* (Wilton, Conn.: Association Press, 1976), p. 12.

5. Awad, p. 136. who in turn attributes it to I. Weiner, "On Incest: A Survey," *Excerpt. Criminol.* 4 (1964): 137–155.

6. J. Herman and L. Hirschman, "Father-Daughter Incest," *Signs* (Summer 1977): 739–741.

7. Suzanne Sgroi, Conference on Sexual Abuse of Children, March 1, 1978, Boston College, Boston, Massachusetts.

CHAPTER IX: NEGLECTED VICTIMS

1. *Sexual Abuse of Children,* Queen's Bench Foundation, 1976, Table I, p. 46.

2. J. T. Landis, "Experiences of 500 Children with Adult Sexual Deviation," *Psychiatric Quarterly Supplement* 30 (1956): 91–109.

3. Information in this paragraph from D. J. West, *Homosexuality Re-Examined* (Minneapolis: University of Minnesota Press, 1977), p. 216–217.

4. Sergeant Lloyd Martin, Los Angeles Police Department's Sexually Exploited Child Unit, as quoted in "How Ruses Lure Victims to Child Pornographers," *Chicago Tribune,* 17 May 1977. Reprinted in *Sexual Exploitation of Children,* the proceedings from the hearings before the Subcommittee on Crime, House of Representatives, Serial #12, 95th Cong., 1st. Sess., USGPO, Washington, D.C., 1977.

5. A. Nicholas Groth and J. Birnbaum, "Adult Sexual Orientation and Attraction to Underage Persons," *Archives of Sexual Behavior,* Vol. 7: 3 (1978): 178, Table I.

6. A. P. Bell and M. S. Weinberg, *Homosexualities: A Study of Human Diversity* (New York: Simon & Schuster, 1978).

7. Los Angeles Police Department, as reported in "Child Pornography: Sickness for Sale," *Chicago Tribune,* May 15, 1977.

CHAPTER X: PEDERASTY—CONTACTS WITH TEEN-AGE MALES

1. Unless otherwise indicated, material in this chapter is from P. Rossman, *Sexual Experience between Men and Boys* (Wilton, Conn.: Association Press, 1976).

2. Ibid., pp. 16–32. See Rossman's book for a much more detailed description of these types.

3. Ibid., p. 91.

4. See, for example, Richard Farson, *Birthrights* (New York: Macmillan, 1974), p. 153.

CHAPTER XI: MOLESTATION

1. See, for example, the study by the San Francisco Police Department in *Sexual Abuse of Children*, Queen's Bench Foundation, 1976, p. 46, in which, of forty-two male victims, 62 percent are nine years and under and 35 percent are ten to seventeen years of age (one to five years, 19 percent; six to nine years, 43 percent; ten to thirteen years, 24 percent; fourteen to seventeen years, 14 percent).

2. A. P. Bell and C. S. Hall, *The Personality of a Child Molester* (Chicago: Aldine, 1971), p. 76.

3. *Boston Globe,* 26 February 1978, p. 13.

4. *Boston Globe,* 27 May 1978.

5. Ann W. Burgess et al., *Sexual Assault of Children and Adolescents* (Lexington, Mass.: Lexington Books, 1978), pp. 14–15.

6. *Boston Globe,* 29 March 1978, p. 4.

7. *Boston Globe,* 25 April 1978, p. 8.

8. P. Rossman, *Sexual Experience between Men and Boys* (Wilton, Conn.: Association Press, 1976), pp. 222–224.

CHAPTER XII: MALE SEX RINGS

1. R. Lloyd, *For Money or Love* (New York: Vanguard Press, 1976), p. xvi. For a general view of the problem recently, see also R. M. Press, "Sexual abuse of boys: a neglected problem," in *Christian Science Monitor,* 14 January 1977, p. 8.

2. See statement of Robin Lloyd (item B-2 in Appendix B) in the House Hearings (Serial No. 12), p. 331 (Note 4, chapter IX).

3. *Time,* 28 November 1977, p. 23.

4. For newspaper accounts see the *Boston Globe* from 11 November 1977, through 2 May 1978.

5. P. Rossman, *Sexual Experience between Men and Boys* (Wilton, Conn.: Association Press, 1976), p. 38.

6. *Boston Globe,* 20 December 1977, p. 2.

7. Mark Rowland, "The Revere Case: Not What It Was Cracked Up to Be," article in *The Real Paper,* 5 August 1978, p. 20.

8. P. Harris, "The Boston Hustling Scene," *The Real Paper,* 29 July 1978, p. 15.

9. Rowland, p. 21.

10. *Boston Globe,* 10 December 1977, p. 3.

11. For one comment on the judge's behavior, see David Farrell, "Justice Bonin's Chutzpa." *Boston Globe,* 10 April 1978.

12. D. J. West, *Homosexuality Re-examined* (Minneapolis: University of Minnesota Press, 1977), p. 211.

13. *New York Times,* 18 November 1973, p. 18.

14. *New York Times,* 4 May 1972, p. 44. Also, 23 May 1972.

15. *Time,* 5 June 1972.

16. Lloyd, p. 40.

CHAPTER XIII: KIDDIE PORN

1. Additional views of Mr. Hatch can be found in *Report of the Committee on the Judiciary,* U.S. Senate on S.1585 (Report No. 95–438), 95th Cong., 1st Sess., USGPO, Washington, D.C., p. 31.

2. See testimony of Sgt. Lloyd Martin, LAPD, reprinted in *Sexual Exploitation of Children,* the proceedings from the hearings (hereinafter referred to as House Hearings) before the Subcommittee on Crime, House of Representatives, Serial #12, 95th Cong., 1st Sess., USGPO, Washington, D.C., 1977, p. 61, which cites the figure as approximately 7 percent. See also H. Dudar, "America Discovers Child Pornography," *Ms.* (August 1977), p. 46, which estimates the figure to be no more than 5 percent.

3. House Hearings, p. 61.

4. D. P. Graunke, "Kiddie Porn," *Plain Truth* (November/December 1977): 17.

5. "Child Pornography: Sickness for Sale," *Chicago Tribune,* 15 May 1977, reprinted in *Protection of Children Against Sexual Exploitation,* the proceedings from the hearings (hereinafter referred to as Senate Hearings) before the Subcommittee to Investigate Juvenile Delinquency of the Committee on the Judiciary of the U.S. Senate, 95th Cong., 1st Sess., USGPO, Washington, D.C., 1978, p. 132.

6. House Hearings, p. 60.

7. *Time,* 4 April 1977, p. 55.

8. *Boston Globe,* 1 August 1978, p. 2.

Notes   177

9. *Washington Post,* "Boy's Farm Scandal," 5 June 1977. Reprinted in House Hearings, pp. 442–443.

10. G. Bliss and M. Sneed, *Chicago Tribune,* no date, reprinted in Senate Hearings.

11. M. Wright, "Porno Ring Uses Church, Tax Laws." *Traverse City* (Mich.) *Record-Eagle.* Reprinted in House Hearings, pp. 82–83. See also pp. 86–88.

12. R. S. Anson, "The Last Porno Show." *New Times.* 24 June 1977. Reprinted in Senate Hearings, p. 154.

13. Testimony of G. Bliss and M. Sneed (Reporters, *Chicago Tribune*), in Senate Hearings, pp. 57–64. See also testimony of investigator J. Lehman, same source, pp. 51–57.

14. *Boston Globe,* 13 October 1977, p. 23.

15. House Hearings, pp. 62–63.

16. Ibid., p. 61.

17. *Boston Globe,* 26 March 1978, p. 2.

18. From *Chicago Tribune,* 16 May 1977. Reprinted in House Hearings, pp. 433–434. See also testimony of B. Carey, State's Attorney for Cook County in Senate Hearings, p. 52.

19. Statement of Robin Lloyd in House Hearings, p. 331.

20. For her testimony, see House Hearings, pp. 42–53.

21. *Time, 28 November 1977, p. 23.*

22. *Boston Globe,* 9 May 1978, p. 4; also 21 May 1978, p. 9.

23. See copy of Sec. 1465 in House Hearings, p. 319.

24. For ACLU testimony, see House Hearings, pp. 121–132. See also Senate Hearings, pp. 97–101.

25. *New York Times. The Report of the Commission on Obscenity and Pornography.* Bantam, 1970, p. 27.

26. *Washington Star,* 11 April 1977, in House Hearings, p. 426.

27. *The Report of the Commission on Obscenity and Pornography,* p. 27.

28. Ibid., p. 32.

29. Technical Report of the Commission on Obscenity and Pornography, Vol. VII: *Erotica and Antisocial Behavior* (Washington, D.C.: USGPO, 1970), p. 280.

30. Ibid., p. 284.

31. Ibid., p. 279.

32. *The Report of the Commission on Obscenity and Pornography,* p. 31.

33. *Erotica and Antisocial Behavior,* p. 250. However, see statement by D. Bremner of Hawaii, in House Hearings, p. 477, claiming rape in Denmark has increased 140 percent in 8 years.

34. Ibid., p. 169.

35. Report 95–438. Report of the Committee on the Judiciary, U.S. Senate on S1585, 95th Cong., 1st Sess., USGPO, Washington, D.C., p. 9.

CHAPTER XIV: VIOLENCE—THE ULTIMATE OBSCENITY

1. Gloria Steinem, *Ms.* (August 1977): 43.

2. Phyllis Chesler, *About Men* (New York: Simon & Schuster, 1978), p. 229.

3. Dworkin, as quoted by Chesler in *About Men,* p. 233.

4. Article, *U-U (Unitarian Universalist) World,* 15 April 1978, p. 9.

5. Steinem editorial, p. 44.

6. *Boston Globe,* 1 May 1978, p. 13.

7. *Boston Globe,* 22 January 1978, p. A6.

8. *American Orthopsychiatric Association Newsletter* (Summer 1978): 19.

9. Ibid.

10. W. A. Schmidt, "Incestuous Behavior as an Etiological Factor Leading to Juvenile Delinquency and Crime," *Child Abuse Conference Proceedings,* Children's Hospital National Medical Center, February 1977, p. 92.

11. D. H. Browning and B. Boatman, "Incest: Children at Risk," *American Journal of Psychiatry* (January 1977): 70, Table I.

12. Suzanne Sgroi, "Child Sexual Assault: Some Guidelines for Intervention and Assessment," in Burgess et al., *Sexual Assault of Children and Adolescents* (Lexington, Mass.: Lexington Books, 1978), p. 136.

13. A. N. Groth, remarks at conference on Sexual Abuse of Children, 1 March 1978, Boston College.

14. *Binghamton (New York) Press.* 21 October 1977, p. 5A.

CHAPTER XV: CHILD PROSTITUTION

1. *Time,* 28 November 1977: 23.

2. *Boston Globe.* 11 November 1977, p. 11.

3. See note 1.

4. M. E. Cahill, "Sexually Abused Children: Fact, Not Fiction," in House Hearings, p. 359.

5. *Boston Globe,* 26 January 1978, pp. 1, 9.

6. Ellen Goodman, "Prostitution and the Law," *Boston Globe,* 3 February 1978, p. 19.

7. See Robert Geiser, "The Rights of Children," *Hastings Law Journal* (March 1977): 1034–1039.

8. R. Lloyd, *For Money or Love* (New York: Vanguard Press, 1976).

9. Testimony of L. H. Martin, LAPD in House Hearings, p. 57.

10. Lloyd, p. 12.

11. Martin, p. 59.

12. P. Rossman, *Sexual Experience between Men and Boys* (Wilton, Conn.: Association Press, 1976), p. 12.

13. Lloyd, p. 112, quoting Martin Hoffman, *The Gay World* (New York: Basic Books, 1968).

14. J. Gerassi, *The Boys of Boise* (New York: Macmillan, 1966), p. 32.

15. D. J. West, *Homosexuality Re-Examined* (Minneapolis: University of Minnesota Press, 1977), p. 223.

16. Philip Harris, "The Boston Hustling Scene," *The Real Paper,* 29 July 1978, p. 15.

CHAPTER XVI: THE CASES OF TWO MALES

1. The material for this and the next chapter has been adapted from an article by the author that appeared in print elsewhere. It has been especially revised and edited for this book. The original source is R. L. Geiser and Sister M. Norberta, "Sexual Disturbance in Young Children," *Maternal Child Nursing* (May/June 1976): 187.

CONCLUSION: AN END TO SEXUAL ABUSE?

1. C. Bahn and M. Daly, "Criminal Justice Reform in Handling Child Sex Abuse," from the *Child Abuse Conference Proceedings,* Children's Hospital National Medical Center, Washington, D.C., February 18–20, 1977, p. 143.

2. *Boston Globe,* 1 October 1978, p. 1.

3. The example comes from R. DeVine, "Sexual Abuse—Who Cares?" from *Conference Proceedings* (Note 1), p. 82.

4. Queen's Bench Foundation. *Sexual Abuse of Children* (1976). Also *Medical Management of Sexually Abused Children and Adolescents* (1977); *Sexual Abuse of Children—A Guide for Parents* (1977).

5. Suzanne M. Sgroi, "Comprehensive Examination for Child Sexual Assault," in Burgess et al., *Sexual Assault of Children and Adolescents* (Lexington, Mass.: Lexington Books, 1978), pp. 143–157.

6. D. Stevins and L. Berliner, "Special Techniques for Child Witnesses," mimeo by Center for Women Policy Studies, Suite 508, 2000 "P" Street, NW, Washington, D.C. 20036.

7. Women Organized Against Rape (WOAR). "Discussing Rape with Children," p. 7.

8. A. A. Rosenfeld, "Sexual Abuse of Children," *Journal of the American Medical Association* (7 July 1978): 43.

9. Mark Rowland, "The Revere Case," *The Real Paper,* 5 August 1978, p. 22.

10. "Some Violence Statistics," *American Psychological Association Monitor* (February 1978): 4.

11. *Boston Globe,* 24–30 September 1978.

Selected Bibliography

BOOKS

Bell, Alan P., and Hall, Calvin S. *The Personality of a Child Molester.* Aldine: 1971.

Bell, Alan P., and Weinberg, M. S. *Homosexualities: A Study of Human Diversity.* Simon & Schuster, 1978.

Burgess, Ann W., Groth, A. Nicholas, et al. *Sexual Assault on Children and Adolescents.* Lexington Books, 1978.

Burgess, Ann W., and Holmstrom, L. L. *Rape! Victims of Crisis.* R. J. Brady Co., 1974.

Gerassi, J. *The Boys of Boise.* Macmillan, 1966.

Lloyd, Robin. *For Money or Love.* Vanguard, 1976.

Meiselman, Karin C. *Incest.* Jossey-Bass, 1978.

Olsen, Jack. *The Man with the Candy.* Simon & Schuster, 1974.

Protection of Children Against Sexual Exploitation. Hearings before the Subcommittee to Investigate Juvenile Delinquency of the Committee on the Judiciary of the U.S. Senate, 95th Cong., 1st. Sess., GPO, Washington, D.C., 1978.

Rossman, Parker. *Sexual Experience Between Men and Boys.* Association Press, 1976.

Sexual Exploitation of Children. Hearing before the Subcommittee on Crime, House of Representatives, Serial #12, 95th Cong., 1st. Sess., GPO, Washington, D.C., 1977.

Stoller, Robert J. *Perversion: The Erotic Form of Hatred.* Pantheon Books, 1975.

Walters, David R. *Physical and Sexual Abuse of Children.* Indiana University Press, 1975.

West, D. J. *Homosexuality Re-Examined.* University of Minnesota Press, 1977.

ARTICLES

Geiser, Robert, and Norberta, Sister Mary. "Sexual Disturbance in Young Children." *Maternal Child Nursing.* May/June 1976.

Gentry, Charles E. "Incestuous Abuse of Children: The Need for an Objective View." *Child Welfare.* June 1978.

Kaufman, Irving, et al. "The Family Constellation and Overt Incestuous Relations between Father and Daughter." *Amer. J. Orthopsychiatry.* 24 (1954).

Kempe, C. Henry, et al. "The Battered-Child Syndrome." *J. Amer. Med. Assoc.* Vol. 181 (1962).

Peters, Joseph J. "Children Who Are Victims of Sexual Assault and the Psychology of Offenders." *Amer. J. Psychotherapy.* July 1976.

Sarafino, Edward P. "An Estimate of Nationwide Incidence of Sexual Offenses Against Children." *Child Welfare.* February 1979.

Schultz, LeRoy G. "The Child Sex Victim." *Child Welfare.* March 1973.

Schultz, LeRoy G. "The Sexual Abuse of Children and Minors: A Bibliography." *Child Welfare.* March 1979.

Sexual Abuse of Children. Queen's Bench Foundation. 1976. 244 California St., Suite 210, San Francisco, Calif. 94111.

Sgroi, Suzanne M. "Sexual Molestation of Children." *Children Today.* May/June 1975.

Summit, Roland, and Kryso, JoAnn. "Sexual Abuse of Children: A Clinical Spectrum." *Amer. J. Orthopsychiatry.* April 1978.

Index